The

HEROIC

FIGURE

The

HEROIC
FIGURE

Essays by
Linda L. Cathcart and Craig Owens

Contemporary Arts Museum
Houston, Texas

Lenders to the Exhibition

Ellen Carey
Dannheisser Foundation
Elaine and Werner Dannheisser
Nancy Graves
Mr. and Mrs. Aron B. Katz
Donald M. Levy M.D., Milwaukee, Wisconsin
Robert Longo
Richard Prince
David Salle
Lenore and Herbert Schorr
Cindy Sherman
Dr. Marylou Solbrig, San Francisco, California
Arthur Solway, New York
Jerry and Emily Spiegel
Mr. and Mrs. Bagley Wright
Private Collections

Brooke Alexander, Inc., New York
Mary Boone Gallery, New York
Xavier Fourcade, Inc., New York
Metro Pictures, New York
Robert Miller Gallery, New York
Semaphore Gallery, New York
Texas Gallery, Houston

Artists in the Exhibition

John Ahearn
Ellen Carey
William Crozier
Nancy Dwyer
Jedd Garet
Thomas Lawson
Robert Longo
Robert Mapplethorpe
Richard Prince
David Salle
Julian Schnabel
Cindy Sherman
Michael Zwack

Preface and Acknowledgements

Since its founding in 1948, the goal of the Contemporary Arts Museum has been to present exhibitions of the current time. During the past thirty-six years, the institution has mounted a variety of exhibitions addressing current issues, and this exhibition is part of a continuing series of major exhibitions devoted to current and traditional topics in American art. *The Heroic Figure* focuses on fifty-five works by thirteen artists and, like other exhibitions in the series, *The Americans: The Landscape,* 1981, *The Americans: The Collage,* 1982 and *American Still Life 1945-1983,* its purpose is to examine a historically important theme and its treatment by contemporary artists.

American figurative art seen in the 1980s reflects both the old and the new in its content, form and style. If it has a unique and new quality, it is a result of this assimilation of old and new imagery. We have wanted very much to compare our new imagery to that produced in Europe—to claim it is newer, more unique and thus better. Can this be possible? It seems that the art produced at any particular time can only be a reflection of its culture and probably cannot be more original or better than any other art either past or from another place.

The relationship between American and European art of our period seems to be a large, critical issue. To me, however, by asking the questions which identify this art as particularly American again removes this exhibition from that question as it does from the one of style. These figures, these heroes, can only be American, produced by Americans.

This exhibition had been organized originally under the sponsorship of the United States Information Agency to represent the United States at the 17th São Paulo Bienale. Due to a series of misunderstandings and changes in posture on the part of the Bienale committee in Brazil, it was not possible to have this exhibition presented in São Paulo. The USIA arranged a tour to Rio de Janeiro, Brazil and Santiago, Chile for the exhibition and the show for which this catalogue was made is an expanded and updated version of that organized about two years ago. The USIA has graciously permitted us the use of all the research and technical materials from that effort and we are grateful to them for that.

This exhibition for Houston was made possible with the cooperation, support and patience of numerous individuals. The staff at the Contemporary Arts Museum performed tirelessly to accomplish the many details critical to the exhibition's organization. I am especially grateful to Emily Croll, Registrar, for coordinating the shipping and packing arrangements; Marti Mayo, Curator, for critical evaluation; Michael Barry, Head Preparator, for his technical expertise; and Emily L. Todd, Curatorial Intern, who researched and compiled the bibliography and assisted in all aspects of the catalogue preparation. Cheryl Blissitte and Pamela Wolfson diligently prepared the manuscript for publication. Special thanks to Laura Catalano for gathering materials, organizing various aspects of the exhibition and for her work on the original catalogue and to Karen Lee Spaulding for editorial assistance.

I am particularly pleased that Craig Owens has agreed to offer us an essay for this catalogue. His discussion of the anti-hero as well as the hero gives a new dimension to this document. He is an acute and longtime observer of the work of these artists and his essay adds to our knowledge and enjoyment of their work.

We have received help from many people and want particularly to acknowledge the generosity of the lenders whose works are included in this exhibition.

The galleries involved have been especially generous with their time and efforts in helping secure loans, locate photographs and provide information. My thanks to: Brooke Alexander and Ted Bonin, Brooke Alexander, Inc.; Fredericka Hunter, Ian Glennie and Kathleen Crain, Texas Gallery; Xavier Fourcade and Margaret Parker, Xavier Fourcade, Inc.; Barry Blinderman, Semaphore Gallery; Robert Miller, John Cheim, Nathan Kernan, Howard Read and Sally Heller, Robert Miller Gallery; Tina Summerlin assistant to Robert Mapplethorpe; Janelle Reiring, Helene Winer and Jim Shepard, Metro Pictures; Mary Boone, Stephen Frailey and Susan Inglett, Mary Boone Gallery; Arnold Glimcher, The Pace Gallery; and Candy Coleman, assistant to Julian Schnabel.

I owe a large debt of gratitude to the participating artists. Their enthusiasm, patience and cooperation in all aspects of the exhibition are essential and have been much appreciated. Robert Mapplethorpe made a special contribution to this catalogue by taking portraits of each of his fellow artists, making an especially beautiful record of this time.

Finally we are pleased to be joined by three museums in this effort. Richard Gruber, Acting Director, Memphis Brooks Museum of Art; Sheila Stewart, Director, Alexandria Museum/Visual Arts Center; and Richard V. West, Director, Santa Barbara Museum of Art will exhibit *The Heroic Figure* in their museums and their staffs and Trustees share our delight in presenting this exhibition.

Linda L. Cathcart
Director

The Heroic Figure
Linda L. Cathcart

The Heroic Figure is an exhibition which attempts not to survey a general tendency in recent art or to define a specific movement or style but rather to focus on the art of thirteen artists who work in different methods and approaches toward figurative imagery for the same purpose. The original idea had been to call this exhibition "Heroes" to bring attention to this aspect of figuration; but it was thought that confusion would arise as to whether the title referred to the artists or their work. Thus *The Heroic Figure* came about, more clearly and aptly describing the intention in presenting these diverse bodies of work.

These thirteen artists, included in this exhibition of art which records the real world, are bound together by some commonalities; all reside in New York City, all have developed mature styles and consummate skills in drawing, modeling or photography within the last ten years and, most importantly, all share a commitment to portrayal of the heroic, monumental figure. Chosen as much for their differences as for their similarities, they range from Cindy Sherman to Julian Schnabel and work in the mediums of painting, sculpture and photography.

Each artist in the exhibition is concerned with direct observation. In this way their art is, indeed, tied to the so-called realist tradition in American art. The artists use models, sometimes themselves, and/or figures taken from secondary sources found in the media. It would be unproductive to take the works in this exhibition and divide them into categories by style. Each shares but one concern and that is the search for the heroic figure. Each artist utilizes his or her own personal symbology to find expression of that form. Sometimes the results are intellectually detached, other times, self-conscious. Each, however, is aware of the social structure of our current culture.

What is presented here is a new understanding and interpretation of the recent figurative tradition. While its origins can be found in that of the European Old Masters, this new figuration is affected specifically by contemporary American culture, and often by media images from television, film, newspapers and magazines. The hero and the heroic image come from America's heritage of pioneers and immigrants as presented by the media and not from the image of the physically perfect warrior as seen in European art. This perspective results in images celebrating unconventional "heroes" — for example, women, blacks and those who are not considered, in the traditional sense, "beautiful." It is not pessimistic or anxious, nor is it a conscious effort to revive old styles. It does, rather, encompass life and death issues, a sense of sexuality and an aura of mystery and timelessness. These works, in their deliberate and conscious elimination of context and narrative, belie the sources of their subject matter, which are indeed contemporary. Images are culled from popular society just as those of Pop Art were; these artists, however, do not align themselves with that movement, for they feel that Pop Art was concerned with the signs and emblems of popular culture. They are concerned with a quality of human drama, sometimes tragic, sometimes idealized, but always monumental in scale or impact.

As modern artists found a way to connect the often used subject of the human form more closely to the actual activity of artmaking, they sought to close the gap between art and life. These thirteen artists have not gone in that direction and followed in the footsteps of the Performance and Conceptual artists before them. Rather they are making an art which is larger than life, more clearly defined than before, more powerful, more artful and more concerned with the sublime, with beauty and with heroic gesture.

Interested in communicating this specific point of view, these artists' images are personalized, and thus the communication with the viewer is a personal one. Each artist in this exhibition shares that need to relate somehow to the model or subject (even those whose images are taken from secondary sources) in order to give life to the resulting image. Without this infusion of the artist's spirit, the works would be static and lifeless.

8

Works of artists such as Robert Mapplethorpe and William Crozier have clear art historical references to classic Greek and Roman statuary; others, like those of Cindy Sherman, reflect the tradition of portraiture. Thomas Lawson and John Ahearn celebrate common people as heroes who have survived perhaps not only tragedy and misfortune but also who have managed to sustain themselves in spite of the vicissitudes of daily life. Richard Prince parodies people and the "glamorous" images they can become while Jedd Garet comments on the anonymity of our technological society with his bulky, faceless figures.

In one way this art is very concrete. These artists work only with forms they can see and with images which make sense in relation to their feelings. They do not work with concepts and theories. The objects they produce are important as objects of craft and beauty because these artists are concerned with enduring images.

In much recent art history the notion of who and what is heroic was confused. Duchamp, for example, made an art which was so modest in its scope and presentation that no one could claim for it heroic proportions or ambitions. But nonetheless, Duchamp became a hero for modern artists. Jackson Pollock, another personal, modern hero, made work which was itself heroic in proportions, scale, color, design and intent. It was, however, for the most part abstract, and did not finally make a statement about the human dilemma past that of the artist's. As artists of heroic symbol, these thirteen contemporary artists might be more closely aligned with Picasso. A great humanist, Picasso painted life figures in pictures where often the background or time was secondary to the narrative of human drama and the forces of life as they shaped the physical being. Picasso is both artist-hero and painter of the heroic.

It is tempting to try to explain this new figuration or our new interest in figurative art as a new movement, style or approach to modernism as something we can easily place in a historical context. We want to see it as a part of a pluralism, or as an extension of Pop Art or as a reaction against Minimalism, Conceptualism or Performance art. Somehow, however, it is important to remember that large numbers of active artists are still working in other ways. It is better to recognize that the figurative mode is part of a continuum which has its roots in centuries-old European art and is now informed by the social structures and mores of our current culture and new technology, resulting in images which are indeed new to us.

Sharing the experience of artmaking recalls the workshops and apprenticeship which produced the grand art of the Renaissance. That tradition is seen in the forms of John Ahearn's work: specifically, busts and torsos and most recently, full figures, which conceivably could find their source in the sculpture produced under the patronage of Italian nobility. Ahearn's works, now made in collaboration with Rigoberto Torres, share a number of characteristics with other works in the exhibition, namely that of preservation of or specific reference to actual size or scale of the human form. There is a kind of realism whereby the subjects are recognizable. They are the Blacks and Hispanics of the South Bronx, posed yet natural, lifted from life into art. The artist wishes the images to transcend their original sources for a higher purpose and through this, they become metaphors. Ahearn's is a realism informed by previous art, as well as by the artist's personal experience. He identifies his heroic subjects with the American pioneer struggle. The meaning of his art is involved with the struggle for a place, with the search for an identity. By taking the specific and making it general, through romanticization and realism, he transforms and elevates the ordinary.

Balance, symmetry and beauty are all important elements in Ellen Carey's work. The human body is her subject; the nude male and female figures captured in her black and white large-scale photographs hold contrived poses which are then overlaid by the artist with black, white and grey dots and dashes of paint. The nudes reveal human frailty and mortality. They also suggest procreative energy and possibilities, serving as classical symbols of beauty. Carey's work illuminates the notion that each person is like another, yet in that equality, there exist numerous and infinite differences of appearance. Ultimately, each succumbs to death, the heroic preserved only by the timelessness of the medium.

William Crozier's involvement with his subjects is so intense and exacting that he has made only twelve pieces during the last fifteen years he has been sculpting. Each figure or set of figures is modeled in clay and then cast in bronze. The sculptures are correctly proportioned anatomically and usually slightly smaller—$3/4$ or $5/7$—than life-size. Crozier's figures express desire, longing, aching, searching—all powerful emotions captured by the artist as moments of humanity in exquisitely rendered forms.

Nancy Dwyer sees the human possibilities between the archetypal and the clichéd figure. Therein, for her, lies the mystery. Each canvas holds a figure or several figures — delineated by as few gestures as possible. Each picture is large and sparsely painted. One or two ground colors divide the canvas and the figures are outlined in contrasting paint or materials. They are looming, stark and arrested in an absorbing moment. The figures can often be identified — a policewoman, a businessman, a nurse — figures of authority and symbols of power in our culture.

Jedd Garet's highly stylized and simplified figures are androgynous, half-human in their shapelessness and lack of identifying features. Isolated, either in and of themselves or against a strange, otherworldly landscape, these figures have an eerie, almost frightening presence. They are painted deliberately in a touchingly child-like manner, which evokes a certain sense of innocence and vulnerability. The traditional theme of man against nature — his challenge to become a hero — is exemplified by portraying figures against a landscape.

Can the hero be the artist without the artist being a hero? Cindy Sherman uses herself as subject matter and thus must actually come to grips with that issue, because she herself does not aspire to becoming a cult figure. Large in scale but not life-size, Sherman's pictures have evolved over the past several years to exclude backgrounds, thus eliminating the narrative and movie still-like quality they had previously. They now show only the subject—herself—filling the frame with little other than a quality of light or perhaps a piece of furniture to give a hint to time or place. The issue is not whether Sherman is all these people but rather, who are all these women she portrays? They are large, evocative figures. They are the women of dreams, fantasies and nostalgia who come most likely from the media. Rarely found in history, heroines have recently become prominent in films, where they are strong enough to embody heroic forces.

Robert Longo's heroic images are perhaps more closely identified with modern or popular culture than those of the other artists in this exhibition. Longo desires true monumentality. The figures in his works are always larger than life. They are the heroes of the type found in magazines, television and film but by collaging images together, Longo creates heroic figures of even greater magnitude. In each situation portrayed by the artist, the figures are engaged in a struggle to remain whole, to retain their identities and to have dignity.

Thomas Lawson often takes his subjects and titles from pictures and headlines found in tabloid newspapers. Lawson's large, square canvases each contain a single or double portrait which look like a newspaper clipping reflected in a mirror. Monochromatic and with no embellishment added, each subject has managed to survive disaster, triumph over a misfortune or, in some unfortunate, tragic instances, been victimized critically. The titles — *Saved, Boy Shot for Bike* and *Battered to Death* — tell us the circumstances and reflect upon the pervasive influence of the media to add a certain poignancy to our perception of these modern, everyday, common heroes.

Robert Mapplethorpe's finely crafted photographs in black and white usually portray a single figure, torso or head. Each nuance of flesh, bone, blood and muscle is as clearly and meticulously recorded as any classical nude rendering. Today our culture is excessively aware and preoccupied with the notion of the beautiful body and of physical fitness. We have awakened to the needs of our physical selves after a decade of interest in our psychological selves. These pictures of male and female, black and white, street people and movie stars, offer new possibilities, while still recalling the classical tradition, for the female and male figures as art objects. Each figure, though, is equalized by the same approach, through technique and style.

Richard Prince uses, for the source of his works, already-generated images from advertisements. These advertisements represent ''perfect'' men or women and were created to tell the consumer how to look and what to aspire to. The objects advertised in these pictures are the trappings for the ideal life. He often chooses to exclude surroundings, background or text isolating the figures; thus, these examples of perfection are removed from their context. Here, too, the works are media-inspired, extolling and caricaturing cultural, consumer heroes. The media thus loses its power for reality and the art gains realism by its selection from contemporary life.

David Salle's pictures are large in size, huge in scale and are often diptychs or triptychs. One panel often contains several floating and layered images of people. Like the mythical images of gods and goddesses which are transfigured from one form to another, these people portrayed are elusive, mysterious and enduring. In the other panels of the pictures Salle will frequently refer to a specific period of art history; for example, in *Zeitgeist Painting #2,* Picasso is recalled by the inclusion of a Cubist guitar. Salle was once asked if his work were to be considered a vehicle, what kind would it be? He answered that it would be a chariot. To the same question regarding religion, he answered Catholic.[1] Aside from the obvious implications and references to classical times and to Catholicism, the most stringent of doctrines, there is also in this work, the worship of heroic figure or deed which religion and mythology can bring to art.

Julian Schnabel seeks to tie his work to meaningful contexts. His is an art which ''seeks to equal what it admires most — great museum art . . . .''[2] Schnabel is reminiscent of the fifties and sixties artists who are perceived as heroic figures; like de Kooning and Rauschenberg who are able to put aside differences between themselves, their lives and their art, Schnabel achieves an art which is more heroic than its maker's myth. Schnabel paints from modern and historical heroic subjects—for example, he uses as subject St. Francis, Venus, Leda and the Swan, Voltaire, Milton, doctors, other artists, even God. His affection for monumental images and stories are part of his search for a timeless imagery and subject matter.

Michael Zwack's figures are isolated from their stories. Like the other artists exhibited here, he casts aside the use of narrative to convey meaning; instead, the meaning is found in the single figure itself. Large and powerfully portrayed, the disconnected images call upon the viewer's repository of experiences and memories to bring meaning to the work. It is particularly unique that we share with these artists enough experiences to ensure an aesthetic response to these singular images. The timelessness of the works, however, rests in their beauty and evocation of elemental human response.

This new heroic art seeks for itself the classical virtues of harmony and beauty, perfection and natural spirit; unlike the Abstract Expressionists who purported to do this with abstract images, these artists seek them through figuration. This is an art which seeks to turn paint, bronze and photography into flesh. It can be soft and expressive, anguished and sometimes even completely silent, but rarely is it despairing. It aspires to be universal and therefore, finally, optimistic.

Some have identified this American generation as one whose voice expresses powerlessness, anxiety, depression and perhaps, even an apocalypse. I think, in opposite terms, that it appears that given a new conservatism, artists are answering with the beautiful, with the sublime, the strong, the unfaltering, and are presenting an art which is not political and not positioned and not an answer, but rather a challenge. That challenge is one of heroism and is presented in an art that is clear, timeless, death-less, fraught with sexuality, with eroticism and with meaning. This may be an art produced out of crisis, but is not an art about crisis. It is not an art of confrontation; it is a moral art, it is an art of dreams.

Notes:
1 Peter Schjeldahl, "David Salle Interview," *Journal* (Los Angeles), no. 30, vol. 3, Sept.-Oct., 1981, p. 18.
2 Roberta Smith, "Schnabel the Vincible," *The Village Voice* (New York), Nov. 2, 1982, p. 81.

Under Arrest
Craig Owens

The Heroic Figure—to whom (or to what) does this title refer? Is it to the artists represented in the present exhibition, or to the figures they represent? Here we are confronted with a dilemma (indeed, every position we can take on the "new figuration" seems to generate an equally plausible counter-position): every "heroic" artist-figure (Julian Schnabel, for example, who is regarded as "the current impersonation of creative virility and artistic heroism")[1] has an anti-heroic counterpart (in this case, David Salle) who poses not as a hero, but as a victim of reified codes and conventions. Nowhere is this attitude more apparent than in the work of those artists who address our collective fascination with the images of the mass media—what Tom Lawson calls "a fatal attraction:"

> This work is conditioned by an understanding that the insistent penetration of the mass media into every facet of our daily lives has made . . . authentic experience difficult, if not impossible. Our daily encounters with one another, and with nature, our gestures, our speech are so thoroughly impregnated with a rhetoric absorbed through the airwaves that we can have no certain claim to the originality of any one of our actions. . . . We no longer know if we mimic or are mimicked. We flicker around the flame of our desire, loving the comfort of repeating a well-worn language and its well-worn sentiments, fearful of losing all control to that language and the society it represents. We are trapped firmly within the terms of a fatal attraction, unable to say "no" with any conviction.[2]

This sense of inauthenticity, entrapment, lack of originality, loss of control, is mirrored in the iconography of contemporary art: artists today exhibit a marked preference for images not of the hero, but of the victim. Lawson's battered children, Cindy Sherman's pin-ups and centerfolds, Nancy Dwyer's heart-attack victim (the dread *Cholesterol*), John Ahearn's portraits of the Black and Hispanic residents of the South Bronx—for the present exhibition the gallery appears to have become a rogues' gallery. Ahearn, of course, heroicizes his subjects, but with the cheerful optimism of one who does not acknowledge the fact that the activity in which he is engaged has been thoroughly problematized. As is well known, in the mid-19th century the avant-garde assumed the responsibility of representing those who had been denied access to the means of representation—Courbet's stonebreakers, Daumier's street entertainers, Degas' street walkers, Baudelaire's ragpicker . . . . Not that the avant-garde represented the *interests* of these marginal figures; it has long been recognized that what is represented by such images is the artist's sense of his own marginality, exploitation, prostitution. In our own century this avant-garde tradition has been continued primarily by photography: Lewis Hine's immigrants, Walker Evans' share-croppers, Dorothea Lange's migrant mother—all of which belong to a genre which Martha Rosler refers to as "victim photography" (in which we can include, I believe, the majority of photographs of women). However we may feel about this tradition—whether we view victim photography as an antidote to, or as part of the system of oppression that marginalized these figures in the first place—it nevertheless calls our attention to the fact that, in modern society, the victim is, as often as not, represented as a hero (and the hero as a victim).

For heroism is primarily a matter of position. In his essay "Psychopathic Characters on the Stage," Freud (psycho)analyzed the hero-figure as a projection of the subject's desire "to feel and to act and to arrange things according to his desire." The desire to be a hero, then, is a desire to occupy an active, controlling and, as this is valorized in the West, *masculine* position—even when the hero is a heroine. Female heroes are invariably endowed with masculine attributes; in Robert Mapplethorpe's photographs of bodybuilder Lisa Lyon, for example, the woman is fitted out with a panoply of exchangeable phallus-substitutes which enable her to masquerade as both masculine and feminine (but not simultaneously).[3] And the victim is identified with the feminine position; hence, male victims are conventionally represented as emasculated. (Both Schnabel's and Salle's works have been productively discussed in terms of castration anxiety, i.e., fear of becoming woman.)[4]

Some artists, however, challenge the stability of the active/passive opposition, and of the sexual differential that accompanies it: Richard Prince, for example, who occupies the position of subject of the gaze—a position which has been analyzed, in recent feminist film criticism, as active, masculine. Posing as the subject whose desire is entirely caught up in—produced by—the media apparatus, he demonstrates that the spectator is in fact captured, manipulated, *subjected* by the image. Although in his work fascination is dispelled along a serial chain, it is nevertheless a chain that fixates and repeats, stages a compulsive return to the same. Composed of discontinuous images which are themselves dispersed, cut, faded (Prince's images seem to dissolve before our very eyes), punctuated by moments of loss, the series fascinates, fixates, immobilizes.[5]

If Prince occupies the position of subject of the gaze, Cindy Sherman positions herself as the object of the (male) gaze—the place to which women have conventionally been assigned by patriarchy. But she also challenges definitions of that position as an entirely passive one. For Sherman's photographs are generated through acts of posing, a transformation of the subject into a picture in which the subject plays an active part. As Roland Barthes wrote in *Camera Lucida,* "Once I feel myself observed by the lens, I constitute myself in the process of posing, I instantaneously make another body for myself, I transform myself in advance into an image. This transformation is an active one . . . ."[6] Posing is not only an act, but an act of aggression, as the grotesque exaggeration and distortion of conventional notions of femininity in Sherman's recent fashion series demonstrate: in these works, her stance can be described, if not as entirely active, at least as passive-aggressive.

Posing, in fact, is neither active nor passive, but corresponds to what is described in grammar as the (reflexive) middle voice. (Every verb in Barthes' account of posing for a photograph is in the middle voice: "constitute myself," "make for myself," "transform myself.") The middle voice is distinguished from both the active and passive by the interiority of the subject to the action implied by the verb; the subject is both subject and object (or, as Barthes wrote, "neither subject nor object, but a subject who feels he is becoming an object.") Thus, pose involves a *splitting* of the subject; as Jacques Lacan observed of the phenomenon of mimetic rivalry, "The being breaks up . . . between its being and its semblance, between itself and that paper tiger it shows to the other."[7]

Contemporary figurative art is an art of *semblance,* of the image in the sense not of picture, but of "public image," facade, paper tiger. The artists represented in the present exhibition are preoccupied with the mask, the masquerade, with disguise and dissimulation (and not simulation, as is often said). Salle, for example, speaks of a "new humanism in art," centered not on the ability of the human subject to transform the world through his actions, but which "views the world as essentially unchangeable except through a *theatricalization* of the terms of our interaction with things and events."[8] Lawson has elaborated a strategy of mimetic rivalry that employs painting as protective coloration in a campaign of art-world "infiltration and sabotage:" "This work," he has written, "chooses to *masquerade* as painting . . . ."[9] Remember that Schnabel is regarded not as the incarnation, but as the *impersonation* of virility and heroism. What we are witnessing, then, is the emergence of an art of *pose*—an art not simply of position and posture, but of imposition, imposture. A certain sense of inauthenticity is always inscribed in the pose.

This tendency manifests itself, first of all, in a preference for broadly theatrical gestures: Robert Longo's wildly gesticulating *Men in the Cities,* for example, who recoil as if from a shot. The gestures of Longo's figures do not appear to emanate from within the figure itself, and therefore to express an intention; rather, they appear to be the product of violent external forces that move, arrange, position the figure, bending it out of shape. Perhaps we should speak, then, of *dis*figuration rather than figuration. As Longo's work illustrates, the essential characteristic of the gesture is not its violence, but its immobility: "What is a gesture?" Jacques Lacan asks in the ninth chapter, titled "What is a Picture?", of *The Four Fundamental Concepts of Psychoanalysis.* "A threatening gesture, for example? It is not a blow that is interrupted. It is certainly something done in order to be arrested and suspended." According to Lacan, this "terminal moment of arrest" is what distinguishes gesture from action, and it is in relation to the former that pictorial creation is to be situated (the gesture according to which the painter deposits paint on canvas).

Two of Nancy Dwyer's paintings illustrate—albeit in a humorous, unself-conscious way that belies their theoretical interest—the relation of the picture to the gesture: *Cholesterol,* which depicts the victim of coronary *arrest,* and *Lady Cop,* in which a figure of authority aims her gun at an (unspecified) target. Both are pictures not simply of other pictures (Dwyer based them on photographs), but of the picture in general and its relation with its viewers. In *Cholesterol*, the frozen, immobilized pose of the victim speaks of the immobility of the image itself, while *Lady Cop* tells of its effect on the viewer. For what Dwyer has represented is not an action—the policewoman does not fire the gun—but a gesture, and a threatening gesture at that, executed with the express purpose of immobilizing her suspect: "Halt! You're under *arrest.*"

According to Lacan, pictures arrest, immobilize their viewers, take them into custody. Thus, the immobility of the image is the source of its fascination, its power over the viewer: the picture does not move with the eye, but brings it to a standstill. Lacan compares the picture's effect with the fight scenes staged by the Peking Opera, which are "punctuated by a series of times of arrest in which the actors pause in a frozen attitude":

> One fights as one has always fought since time immemorial, much more with gestures than with blows. Of course, the spectacle itself is content with an absolute dominance of gestures. In these ballets, no two people ever touch one another, they move in different spaces in which are spread out whole series of gestures, which, in traditional combat, nevertheless have the value of weapons, in the sense that they may well be effective as instruments of intimidation.[10]

The picture as weapon, instrument of intimidation: this has, of course, been the concern of all of Robert Longo's work; hence, his preoccupation with the immobility of the work of art, an immobility which is embodied in the frozen gesture. But Longo is not alone: we could also cite, in this regard, Ellen Carey's gestural overpainting of still photographs, which does not reanimate her posed figures, but further immobilizes them, locks them into place. Or the fact that Schnabel paints what have been described as "intricate, motionless arrangements of dead, lifeless material"[11]—still life.

If the history of painting is regarded as a succession not of styles, but of modes of pictorial signification, each of which posits the relation of the artist to the world differently, then the work in the present exhibition testifies to the emergence of a new mode of pictorial signification, one that is based not on action, but on *gesture.* As is well known, modernism replaced the Renaissance model of the artist as the subject of perception—of art as the imitation, representation, reproduction of Nature—with a model of the artist as producer, of art as production rather than reproduction. The modernist artist was an operational subject engaged in the active transformation of the external world; he was, in fact, endowed with the capacity "to feel and to act and to arrange things according to his desire."[12] Hence modernism's political program: to join forces with science and technology for the transformation of the lived environment according to rational principles of function and utility.

This transitive, transformative, *performative*—in linguistics, a performative statement is one which accomplishes an action ("The meeting is adjourned")—model of pictorial signification culminated in minimalism, in minimalist "task-performance" in particular, in which the performer was reduced to a "neutral doer" (this term is Yvonne Rainer's) entirely absorbed in and defined by the task he or she was called upon to execute. Although condemned (by Michael Fried) as theatrical, minimalist performance was in fact a critique of the narcissistic posturing and projection of persona in conventional modes of theatrical presentation. Minimalism, then, substituted action for gesture; as Rosalind Krauss wrote of Richard Serra's *Hand Catching Lead* (1969)— a three-minute film in which a disembodied hand repeatedly attempts to catch a series of falling metal strips—"As one watches, one shares the real time of the sculptor's concentration on the task and one has the sense that during that time, the artist's body *is* the task: his very being is represented by this outward show of behavior contracted down to a single extremity."[13]

As this passage indicates, what the functional, purely operational model of the artist-subject *represses* is the data of sexuality and the unconscious—the data, that is, of psychoanalysis—and it is precisely this repressed material that has returned in a massive way in the figurative art of the last five years. Hence its affinity with surrealism, the only 20th-century art movement to operate with a psychoanalytic theory of desire. The surrealist artist-subject was neither the perceptual subject—the passive recipient of data from the external world—nor the operational subject—the active transformer of that world—but instead the *desiring* subject, the subject of the unconscious.

However, the substitution in contemporary art of gesture for action, as well as the predominance of pose, suggest another affinity. Recently, English music critic Simon Frith has spoken of the "triumph," in popular music, of a "Pop sensibility," referring to the eclipse of the rock musician by the pop star (Bowie, Boy George). Frith characterizes this sensibility according to a series of substitutions: of gesture for action, style for politics, artifice for authenticity . . . .[14] Frith's argument is revealing in the context of the present exhibition, for these artists owe an enormous, if unacknowledged debt to Andy Warhol, who proposed a new model of the artist-subject — the artist as a poseur. Warhol refused the active model of the artist-subject in favor of a provocative passivity; he adopted the serialized production techniques of the culture industry; he was preoccupied with mask and the masquerade; above all, Warhol was obsessed with stillness, immobility. In 1964 Warhol produced an eight-hour film in which a static camera filmed an immovable Empire State Building; "the Empire State Building is a star," Warhol proclaimed. The title of that film is *Empire*. It seems significant that in 1984 Robert Longo should be at work on a film titled *Empire,* which is to "star" Eric Bogosian, a master of vocal disguise and mimetic pose. . . .Perhaps these are the only heroic figures/stars appropriate today.

[1] The Holy Ghost Writers, "Condensation and Dish-Placement," *Real Life Magazine* (New York), no. 9, Winter 1982/83, p. 9. This essay remains the best analysis of Schnabel's work to date.
[2] Thomas Lawson, "A Fatal Attraction," *A Fatal Attraction: Art and the Media* (exhibition catalogue), (Chicago: The Renaissance Society, 1982), p. 3.
[3] See Silvia Kolbowski, "Covering Mapplethorpe's 'Lady'," *Art in America* (New York), vol. 71, no. 6, Summer 1983, pp. 10–11.
[4] See The Holy Ghost Writers.
[5] My account of Prince's work is indebted to Herman Rapaport's excellent essay on Lewis Carroll's photographs of little girls, "The Disarticulated Image: Gazing in Wonderland," *Enclitic* (Minneapolis), vol. 6, no. 2, Fall 1982, pp. 57–77.
[6] Roland Barthes, *Camera Lucida* (New York: Hill & Wang, 1981), p. 14.
[7] Jacques Lacan, *The Four Fundamental Concepts of Psychoanalysis* (New York: Norton, 1978), p. 107.
[8] "Images That Understand Us: A Conversation with David Salle and James Welling," *Journal* (Los Angeles), no. 27, vol. 3, June-July 1980, p.44.
[9] Thomas Lawson, "Too Good to Be True," *Journal* (Los Angeles), no. 33, vol. 4, Summer 1982, p. 43.
[10] Lacan, pp. 116–17.
[11] The Holy Ghost Writers, p. 12.
[12] For a more detailed treatment of this material, see Jean-Joseph Goux, *Les Iconoclastes* (Paris: Seuil, 1978), pp. 129–43.
[13] Rosalind Krauss, *Passages in Modern Sculpture* (New York: Viking, 1977), pp. 276, 279.
[14] Frith's remarks were made during a conference, *Marxism and the Interpretation of Culture,* held at the University of Illinois, Champagne/Urbana in July 1983.

Catalogue of the Exhibition

All dimensions are given in inches and centimeters with height preceding width, preceding depth.

John Ahearn
with Rigoberto Torres

Norma and Mario 1981
Painted cast plaster
24 x 16 x 8 in. (60.96 x 40.64 x 20.32 cm.)
Courtesy Brooke Alexander, Inc., New York

Duane and Al 1982
Painted cast plaster
33 x 32 x 10 in. (83.82 x 81.28 x 25.40 cm.)
Courtesy Brooke Alexander, Inc., New York

Pat 1982
Painted cast plaster
28¹/2 x 16¹/2 x 11 in. (72.39 x 41.91 x 27.94 cm.)
Courtesy Brooke Alexander, Inc., New York

Thomas 1983
Painted cast plaster
46 x 29 x 7 in. (116.84 x 73.66 x 17.78 cm.)
Collection Lenore and Herbert Schorr
Courtesy Brooke Alexander, Inc., New York
*

Ellen Carey

DNA 1981
Mixed media on photograph
39¹/4 x 29¹/4 in. (99.70 x 74.30 cm.)
Collection Nancy Graves

Grey Falling 1982
Mixed media on photograph
39 x 29 in. (99.06 x 73.66 cm.)
Courtesy the artist and Texas Gallery, Houston

Spirals Change 1982
Mixed media on photograph
62 x 81 in. (157.48 x 205.74 cm.)
Collection Arthur Solway, New York

Warp 1982
Mixed media on photograph
41¹/2 x 37¹/2 in. (105.41 x 95.25 cm.)
Collection Dr. Marylou Solbrig, San Francisco, California

Dark Light 1983
Mixed media on photograph
54 x 84 in. (137.16 x 213.36 cm.)
Courtesy the artist and Texas Gallery, Houston
*

William Crozier

Bob and Brenda 1975-80
Bronze, ed. 4/9
52 x 60 x 40 in. (132.08 x 152.40 x 101.60 cm.)
Courtesy Xavier Fourcade, Inc., New York

Marilyn 1975-80
Bronze, ed. 3/9
38 x 44¹/2 x 34 ³/4 in. (96.52 x 113.03 x 88.27 cm.)
Courtesy Xavier Fourcade, Inc., New York
*

Aching 1980-81
Bronze, ed. 3/9
52 x 50¹/2 x 91 in. (132.08 x 128.70 x 231.14 cm.)
Courtesy Xavier Fourcade, Inc., New York

Dredge 1983
Bronze, ed., 1/9
31¹/2 x 71 x 27¹/2 in. (80.01 x 180.34 x 69.85 cm.)
Courtesy Xavier Fourcade, Inc., New York

Nancy Dwyer

Cholesterol 1982
Acrylic on canvas
48 x 72 in. (121.92 x 182.88 cm.)
Courtesy Semaphore Gallery, New York

Lady Cop 1982
Acrylic on canvas
72 x 48 in. (182.88 x 121.92 cm.)
Courtesy Semaphore Gallery, New York

The Mirror 1983
Acrylic on mirrored Plexiglas and Formica
44¹/4 x 56 x 3 in. (112.40 x 142.24 x 7.62 cm.)
Courtesy Texas Gallery, Houston

War Boys 1983
Aluminum, Formica and lacquer
62¹/4 x 55¹/4 x 5 in. (158.12 x 140.34 x 12.70 cm.)
Courtesy Texas Gallery, Houston
*

Jedd Garet

New Servant (Friend and Enemy) 1981
Painted cast aluminum
47 x 32 x 7 in. (119.38 x 81.28 x 17.78 cm.)
Courtesy Texas Gallery, Houston

The Hero of Redworld 1983
Acrylic on canvas
84 x 105 in. (213.36 x 266.70 cm.)
Collection Donald M. Levy M.D., Milwaukee,
Wisconsin

Mom and Dad Outside 1983
Acrylic on canvas
95 x 70 x 5¹/₂ in. (241.30 x 177.80 x 13.97 cm.)
Collection Mr. and Mrs. Aron B. Katz
*

White Vase 1983
Acrylic on canvas
105 x 84 in. (266.70 x 213.36 cm.)
Collection Elaine and Werner Dannheisser

Thomas Lawson

Battered to Death 1981
Oil on canvas
48 x 48 in. (121.92 x 121.92 cm.)
Courtesy Metro Pictures, New York

Boy Shot for Bike 1981
Oil on canvas
48 x 48 in. (121.92 x 121.92 cm.)
Courtesy Metro Pictures, New York

Saved 1982
Oil on canvas
48 x 96 in. (121.92 x 243.84 cm.)
Courtesy Metro Pictures, New York

To Those Who Follow After 1983
Oil on canvas
60 x 168 in. (152.40 x 426.72 cm.)
Courtesy Metro Pictures, New York
*

Robert Longo

Culture Culture 1982-83
Mixed media
91¹/₂ x 147³/₄ in. (232.41 x 375.29 cm.)
Collection the artist
Courtesy Metro Pictures, New York
*

V 1983-84
Mixed media
129¹/₂ x 114 x 36 in. (328.93 x 289.56 x
91.44 cm.)
Private Collection
Courtesy Metro Pictures, New York

Robert Mapplethorpe

Eighteen Photographs 1982-83
Gelatin silver prints
18 photographs: each 20 x 16 in.
(50.80 x 40.64 cm.)
Courtesy Robert Miller Gallery, New York

Glenn Close 1982
Gelatin silver print
20 x 16 in. (50.80 x 40.64 cm.)
Courtesy Robert Miller Gallery, New York
*

Donald Sutherland 1983
Gelatin silver print
20 x 16 in. (50.80 x 40.64 cm.)
Courtesy Robert Miller Gallery, New York

Ed Ruscha 1984
Gelatin silver print
20 x 16 in. (50.80 x 40.64 cm.)
Courtesy Robert Miller Gallery, New York

Ellen Barkin 1984
Gelatin silver print
20 x 16 in. (50.80 x 40.64 cm.)
Courtesy Robert Miller Gallery, New York

Ellsworth Kelly 1984
Gelatin silver print
20 x 16 in. (50.80 x 40.64 cm.)
Courtesy Robert Miller Gallery, New York
*

Richard Prince

Untitled (Carole) 1982
Color photograph
30 x 44 in. (76.20 x 111.76 cm.)
Courtesy the artist

Untitled (Kristy) 1982
Color photograph
30 x 44 in. (76.20 x 111.76 cm.)
Courtesy the artist

Untitled (Laoura) 1982
Color photograph
30 x 44 in. (76.20 x 111.76 cm.)
Courtesy the artist

Untitled (Luanne) 1982
Color photograph
30 x 44 in. (76.20 x 111.76 cm.)
Courtesy the artist

Untitled (Fayy) 1983
Color photograph
30 x 44 in. (76.20 x 111.76 cm.)
Courtesy the artist
*

Untitled (Russell) 1983
Color photograph
30 x 44 in. (76.20 x 111.76 cm.)
Courtesy the artist
*

David Salle

Zeitgeist Painting #2 1982
Oil and acrylic on canvas
156 x 117 in. (396.24 x 297.18 cm.)
Collection Jerry and Emily Spiegel
(exhibited in Houston and Santa Barbara only)

Concave Warrior 1983
Oil and acrylic on canvas and chair legs
117 x 108 in. (297.18 x 274.32 cm.)
Collection the artist
Courtesy Mary Boone Gallery, New York
*

King Kong 1983
Acrylic and oil on canvas, platform and bulb
123 x 96 x 26 in. (312.42 x 243.84 x 66.04 cm.)
Collection Mr. and Mrs. Bagley Wright
(exhibited in Houston only)

Julian Schnabel

Procession (for Jean Vigo) 1979
Oil on wood
110 x 86 in. (279.40 x 218.44 cm.)
Private Collection, New York
*

Portrait of My Daughter 1982
Plates, bondo and oil on wood
108 x 84 in. (274.32 x 213.36 cm.)
Private Collection, New York

Maria Callas 3 1983
Oil on velvet
108 x 120 in. (274.32 x 304.80 cm.)
Private Collection, New York

Cindy Sherman

Untitled 1982
Color photograph
38 x 24 in. (96.52 x 60.96 cm.)
Courtesy the artist and Metro Pictures,
New York

Untitled 1982
Color photograph
45 1/4 x 30 in. (114.94 x 76.20 cm.)
Courtesy the artist and Metro Pictures,
New York

Untitled 1982
Color photograph
45 1/4 x 30 in. (114.94 x 76.20 cm.)
Courtesy the artist and Metro Pictures,
New York

Untitled 1982
Color photograph
45 1/4 x 30 in. (114.94 x 76.20 cm.)
Courtesy the artist and Metro Pictures,
New York

Untitled 1982
Color photograph
45 1/4 x 30 in. (114.94 x 76.20 cm.)
Courtesy the artist and Metro Pictures,
New York

Untitled 1983
Color photograph
34 3/4 x 16 1/2 in. (88.27 x 41.91 cm.)
Courtesy the artist and Metro Pictures,
New York
*

Untitled 1983
Color photograph
35 1/4 x 21 1/4 in. (89.54 x 53.98 cm.)
Courtesy the artist and Metro Pictures,
New York
*

Michael Zwack

The Last Great Performance 1981
Raw pigment and oil on paper
76 x 71 in. (193.04 x 180.34 cm.)
Collection Dannheisser Foundation
*

Untitled 1982
Raw pigment and oil on paper
79 x 50 in. (200.66 x 127 cm.)
Courtesy Metro Pictures, New York

Untitled 1982
Raw pigment and oil on paper
57 1/2 x 87 1/2 in. (146.05 x 222.25 cm.)
Courtesy Metro Pictures, New York

*These works will be shown in the Alexandria
Museum/Visual Arts Center in an abbreviated
version of the exhibition.

John Ahearn
photograph by Robert Mapplethorpe, March 1983

John Ahearn

All these sculptures are selected from a series of community portraits, lifecasts created and displayed in the South Bronx. All the casting has been done publicly with the active participation of those represented. Most of the casts are later used as sections for permanent sculpture murals in the community. All casting was done with the assistance of Rigoberto Torres and the help of friends. I wish to explore new roles for the artist in society and to develop wider participation in the art process.

Norma and Mario 1981
Painted cast plaster
24 x 16 x 8 in. (60.96 x 40.64 x 20.32 cm.)
Courtesy Brooke Alexander, Inc., New York

Duane and Al 1982
Painted cast plaster
33 x 32 x 10 in. (83.82 x 81.28 x 25.40 cm.)
Courtesy Brooke Alexander, Inc., New York

Pat 1982
Painted cast plaster
28¹/₂ x 16¹/₂ x 11 in. (72.39 x 41.91 x 27.94 cm.)
Courtesy Brooke Alexander, Inc., New York

24

Thomas 1983
Painted cast plaster
46 x 29 x 7 in. (116.84 x 73.66 x 17.78 cm.)
Collection Lenore and Herbert Schorr
Courtesy Brooke Alexander, Inc., New York

25

John Ahearn

One-Artist Exhibitions and Projects
1979
Juvenile Justice Center,
Philadelphia, Pennsylvania.

Fashion/Moda and South
Bronx Hall of Fame, Bronx, New York.

1980
Walton Avenue Sculpture Workshop, Bronx,
New York.

1981-83
Intervale Outdoor Arts Project, Bronx, New
York.

1982
Galerie Rudolf Zwirner, Cologne, West
Germany.

1983
Brooke Alexander, Inc., New York.

Galerie Rudolf Zwirner, Cologne, West
Germany.

Selected Readings
1980
Deitch, Jeffrey. "Report from Times Square."
Art in America (New York), vol. 68, no. 7, Sept.,
pp. 58-63.

Levin, Kim. "The Times Square Show." *Arts
Magazine* (New York), vol. 55, no. 1, Sept.,
pp. 87-89.

Lippard, Lucy. "Sex and Death and Shock and
Schlock: A Long Review of the Times Square
Show." *Artforum* (New York), vol. 19, no. 2,
Oct., pp. 50-55.

Rickey, Carrie. "John Ahearn, New Museum
Windows." *Artforum* (New York), vol. 18, no. 7,
Mar., p. 75.

Robinson, Walter. "John Ahearn at Fashion/
Moda." *Art in America* (New York), vol. 68,
no. 1, Jan., p. 108.

1981
Albright-Knox Art Gallery, CEPA Gallery, and
HALLWALLS, Buffalo, New York. *Figures:
Forms and Expressions*, Nov. 20-Jan. 3, 1982.
Catalogue, texts by G. Roger Denson, Biff
Henrich, Charlotta Kotik and Susan Krane.

"John Ahearn." *Appearances* (New York),
nos. 5 & 6, pp. 116-21.

Larson, Kay. "Sculpting Figuratively." *New York
Magazine* (New York), Nov. 16, p. 122.

Ratcliff, Carter. "The Distractions of Theme."
Art in America (New York), vol. 69, no. 9,
Nov., pp. 19-23.

Ricard, René. "The Radiant Child." *Artforum*
(New York), vol. 20, no. 4, Dec., pp. 35-43.

Schjeldahl, Peter. "Anxiety as a Rallying Cry."
The Village Voice (New York), Sept. 16, p. 86.

1982

Contemporary Arts Center, Cincinnati, Ohio. *Face It: 10 Contemporary Artists*, July 8-Aug. 28. Catalogue, texts by William Olander and Joanna Frueh. Organized by the Ohio Foundation on the Arts. Traveled to The Museums at Hartwick College, Oneonta, New York, Sept. 12-Oct. 16; The College of Wooster Art Museum, Ohio, Oct. 24-Nov. 21; Contemporary Art Center of Cleveland, Ohio, Dec. 3-Jan. 3, 1983; Trisolini Gallery, Ohio University, Athens, Jan. 10-Feb. 12, 1983; University of Colorado Art Galleries, Boulder, Mar. 5-Apr. 9, 1983; Freedman Galleries, Albright College, Reading, Pennsylvania, Mar. 17-June 19, 1983; Doane Hall Art Galleries, Allegheny College, Meadville, Pennsylvania, Oct. 20-Nov. 18, 1983; Southern Ohio Museum and Cultural Center, Portsmouth, Dec. 18, 1983-Jan. 28, 1984.

DeAk, Edit. "John Ahearn: We Are Family." *Artforum* (New York), vol. 21, no. 3, Nov., pp. 73-74.

Goldstein, Richard. "Art Beat: Something That Loves a Wall." *The Village Voice* (New York), Aug. 3, p. 31.

Kirshner, Judith Russi. "74th American Exhibition, Art Institute of Chicago." *Artforum* (New York), vol. 21, no. 2, Oct., pp. 74-76.

Lippard, Lucy R. "Art: Revolting Issues." *The Village Voice* (New York), July 27, p. 75.

Milwaukee Art Museum, Wisconsin. *New Figuration in America*, Dec. 3-Jan. 23, 1983. Catalogue, texts by Russell Bowman and Peter Schjeldahl.

Siegel, Jeanne. "The New Reliefs." *Arts Magazine* (New York), vol. 56, no. 8, Apr., pp. 140-44.

_____. "New York: Figuratively Sculpting, P.S. 1." *Art Express* (Providence, Rhode Island), vol. 2, no. 2, Mar.-Apr., p. 64.

1983

Dimitrijevic, Nena. "Urban Kisses, Institute of Contemporary Arts, London." *Flash Art* (Milan, Italy), no. 110, Jan., p. 66.

Glatt, Cara. "Sculptors Look at Human Form." *The Chicago Herald* (Chicago), May 25, p. 10.

Glueck, Grace. "John Ahearn and Rigoberto Torres." *The New York Times* (New York), July 1, p. C19.

Goldstein, Richard. "Artbeat: The Politics of Culture." *The Village Voice* (New York), July 26, p. 37.

_____. "Heros and Villains: In the Belly of the Bronx." *The Village Voice* (New York), Jan. 4.

Kuspit, Donald B. "New Figuration in America at the Milwaukee Art Museum." *Art in America* (New York), vol. 71, no. 8, Sept., pp. 178-79.

Larson, Kay. "John Ahearn." *New York Magazine* (New York), Aug. 1, p. 64.

Moser, Charlotte. "Renaissance Show Surveys Ten Years of Using Human Form in Sculpture." *Chicago Sun-Times* (Chicago), May 29, Show section, p.6.

Murray, Megan. "Casting Director." *New York Daily News* (New York), Sunday News Magazine, July 3.

"Openings: John Ahearn." *Esquire* (New York), vol. 100, no. 2, Aug., p. 111.

The Renaissance Society at the University of Chicago, Illinois. *The Sixth Day: A Survey of Recent Developments in Figurative Sculpture*, May 8-June 15. Catalogue, text by Richard Flood.

Shepard, Joan. "Artistic Immortality for Ordinary People." *New York Daily News* (New York), Metro section, July 30.

Storr, Robert. "John Ahearn and Rigoberto Torres at Brooke Alexander." *Art in America* (New York), vol. 71, no. 10, Nov., pp. 226-27.

1984

San Francisco Museum of Modern Art, California. *The Human Condition: SFMMA Biennial III*, June 28-Aug. 26. Catalogue, texts by Dorothy Martinson, Wolfgang Max Faust, Achille Bonito Oliva, Klaus Ottmann, Edward Kienholz.

Ellen Carey
photograph by Robert Mapplethorpe, March 1983

Ellen Carey

The photograph is a captured reality. It holds an image in a machine-made likeness, the epitome of a technological illusion of immortality. Photographs never die. They massage the human dilemma in its chronic diagnosis: the duality of body and soul.

The body is finite. Human beings exist day-to-day with anxious dread, conscious of the leveling experiences of time. How do we maintain spiritual equanimity? Longing for infinity, man creates. This act of faith denies death.

Detached from color, the images rely on the lush variants of all color — black and white. Invoking stellar mystery and classicism, the primal elements of the painting both conceal and protect the photographs. As a point of departure, the photographs are also a screen, a surface for astral projections. Abstracted over the hyper-reality of the figures, the vortexes of fear, black holes of mistaken perceptions, the swirls and spirals of life's contradictions co-exist in a never ending helix of reality and dreams. My dots and dashes evoke the ancient practice of body decoration. Nudes also suggest that "sex is an inevitable component of man's confusion over the meaning of his life, a meaning split hopelessly into two realms — symbols (freedom) and body (fate)."[1] The dichotomy is the picture.

[1] Ernest Becker, *The Denial of Death* (New York: The Free Press, 1973), p. 44.

DNA 1981
Mixed media on photograph
39¹/₄ x 29¹/₄ in. (99.70 x 74.30 cm.)
Collection Nancy Graves

Grey Falling 1982
Mixed media on photograph
39 x 29 in. (99.06 x 73.66 cm.)
Courtesy the artist and Texas Gallery, Houston

31

Spirals Change 1982
Mixed media on photograph
62 x 81 in. (157.48 x 205.74 cm.)
Collection Arthur Solway, New York

Warp 1982
Mixed media on photograph
41¹/₂ x 37¹/₂ in. (105.41 x 95.25 cm.)
Collection Dr. Marylou Solbrig, San Francisco, California

Dark Light 1983
Mixed media on photograph
54 x 84 in. (137.16 x 213.36 cm.)
Courtesy the artist and Texas Gallery, Houston

Ellen Carey

One-Artist Exhibitions
1978
HALLWALLS, Buffalo, New York.

1981
Concord Gallery, New York.

1982
University Art Museum, University of New Mexico, Albuquerque.

1983
Memorial Union Art Gallery, University of California, Davis.

Selected Readings
1974
Wolfson, Gary. *Young American Photographers Vol. 1*. New York: Lustrum Press.

1977
Albright-Knox Art Gallery, Buffalo, New York. *In Western New York*, Mar. 26-Apr. 17. Catalogue.

Carey, Ellen. "Self Portraits." *Impressions* (Toronto, Ontario, Canada), June, pp. 14-15.

Coleman, A.D. *The Grotesque in Photography*. New York: Ridge Press and Summit Books, pp. 90-93.

The Renaissance Society at the University of Chicago, Illinois. *Recent Portraiture*, Feb. 27-Apr. 2. Catalogue, text by Dennis Adrien.

1978
"Portfolios: Ellen Carey." *Photography Annual 1979* (New York: Popular Photography/Ziff Davis Publishers), pp. 52-55.

1979
Lifson, Ben. "Redundant Kisses, Engaging Ambiguities." *The Village Voice* (New York), June 11, p. 82.

Rice, Shelly. "Image Making." *The Soho Weekly News* (New York), May 24-30, p. 50.

Upton Gallery, State University College, Buffalo, New York. *HALLWALLS: 5 Years*, Nov. 5-15. Catalogue, text by Linda L. Cathcart. Organized by The New Museum, New York. Traveled to A Space, Toronto, Ontario, Canada, Feb. 16-Mar. 8, 1980; Parsons School of Art Gallery, New York, June 20-July 18, 1980.

1980
The Washington Project for the Arts, Washington, D.C. *Painterly Photographs*, Feb. 8-Mar. 1. Catalogue, text by Anthony Bannon.

1981
Albright-Knox Art Gallery, CEPA Gallery, and HALLWALLS, Buffalo, New York. *Figures: Forms and Expressions*, Nov. 20- Jan. 3, 1982. Catalogue, texts by G. Roger Denson, Biff Henrich, Charlotta Kotik and Susan Krane.

Contemporary Arts Museum, Houston, Texas. *The New Photography*, Jan. 17-Feb. 22. Catalogue, texts by Linda L. Cathcart and Marti Mayo.

Kalil, Susie. "Photographic Cross Currents." *Artweek* (Oakland, California), Feb. 7, pp. 1, 16.

The Pratt Manhattan Center, New York. *PhotoFusion*, Jan. 12-31. Catalogue, text by A.D. Coleman.

Rheinisches Landesmuseum, Bonn, West Germany. *Lichtbildnisse: The Portrait in Photography*, Mar. 1-June 1. Catalogue, text by Klaus Honnef.

San Francisco Museum of Modern Art, California. *The Markers*, May 29-July 26. Catalogue, text by Van Deren Coke.

1982
Bannon, Anthony. "An Artists' Place." *Buffalo Evening News* (Buffalo), Jan. 29, p. 3.

The Bronx Museum of the Arts, New York. *Photo Start*, Sept. 14-Dec. 5. Catalogue, text by Philip Verre.

The Santa Barbara Museum of Art, California. *Contemporary Photography as Phantasy*, June 19-Aug. 15. Catalogue, text by Fred Parker.

1983
The Center Gallery, Bucknell University, Lewisburg, Pennsylvania. *Faces Since the 50's*, Mar. 11-Apr. 17. Catalogue, text by Joseph Jacobs.

Knode, Marilu. "Ellen Carey at Pace McGill." *Manhattan Arts* (New York), Oct. 16, p. 3.

Memorial Union Art Gallery, University of California, Davis. *Ellen Carey: Self Portraits*, Nov. 16-Dec. 19. Catalogue.

Moufarrege, Nicholas. "Group Show, Olsen Gallery." *Flash Art* (Milan, Italy), no. 114, Nov., p. 69.

"Upcoming Illustrator." *Art Direction* (New York), vol. 34, no. 11, Feb., p. 68.

1984
Naef, Weston and Rathbone, Belinda, ed. *The Gallery of New Photography/New Directions*, Tokyo, Japan: Shueisha Publishing Co., Ltd., p. 144.

William Crozier
photograph by Robert Mapplethorpe, March 1983

William Crozier

Two sculptures presented in this exhibition were started in 1975 and finished in 1980. They were modeled in plasteline and then cast in bronze. Bob and Brenda *is 5/7 life-size and* Marilyn *is full life-size. The sculptures were worked on only with the models present and in response to the models. The concepts grew with the modeling and with interaction of the people involved.*

Both pieces represent a longing and a reaching out for sexual contact as a dynamic of life.

In the sculpture Bob *and* Brenda *the horizontal and vertical forces; the male and female are building their powers through individuality and sexual presentation. The personalities presented are approaching each other through sexual positioning and this implies searching and questioning rather than a sure and defined love attachment. They seem sexually attracted and approaching some solution.*

The sculpture Marilyn *is a reclining woman reaching out and up with her entire self to pull the viewer down and into herself. Very little of her body is touching the ground but she does not want to leave the ground. She has decided on her object of desire and is reaching out with everything for it. She is reaching with arms and legs and head and genitals. The* Bob *and* Brenda *are not decided and retain the horizontal/vertical; while the* Marilyn *has decided and fills the space of the diagonal between the horizontal and vertical.*

The sculpture Aching *is a man 5/7 life-size arching upward on the balls of his feet, trying to get away from himself, off the earth; away from his two shadows that stretch out behind him ominously on a mudlike surface. The larger shadow is male, approximately eight feet long and in low relief. It is modeled after the male model's real shadow as it lay on the studio floor. The second shadow is female, life-size and lies within the other shadow.*

Dredge *is a heroine. The bottom of the river is mud and trash. She insists on moving forward but instead is being dragged by a powerful force. She is being pulled through memory. She is torn by it, but not broken.*

Bob and Brenda 1975-80
Bronze, ed. 4/9
52 x 60 x 40 in. (132.08 x 152.40 x 101.60 cm.)
Courtesy Xavier Fourcade, Inc., New York

Marilyn 1975-80
Bronze, ed. 3/9
38 x 44¹/₂ x 34 ³/₄ in. (96.52 x 113.03 x 88.27 cm.)
Courtesy Xavier Fourcade, Inc., New York

39

Aching 1980-81
Bronze, ed. 3/9
52 x 50¹/₂ x 91 in. (132.08 x 128.70 x 231.14 cm.)
Courtesy Xavier Fourcade, Inc., New York

Dredge 1983
Bronze, ed., 1/9
31¹/₂ x 71 x 27¹/₂ in. (80.01 x 180.34 x 69.85 cm.)
Courtesy Xavier Fourcade, Inc., New York

William Crozier

One-Artist Exhibitions
1981
Xavier Fourcade, Inc., New York.

Richard Hines, Seattle, Washington.

Selected Readings
1973
Rosenbaum, Lee. "Discovered Artist Still Unknown." *Art Workers News* (New York), Dec.

1981
Berlind, Robert. "Recent Realism and the Artists Choice Museum." *Art Journal* (New York), vol. 41, no. 2, Summer, p. 179.

Kramer, Hilton. "Sculptors Who Triumph in Bronze." *The New York Times* (New York), May 24, pp. D25, D35.

Smith, Roberta. "Seductive Selections." *The Village Voice* (New York), June 10, p. 89.

1983
Artner, Alan G. "The return of the human touch: Figurative sculpture is really back in vogue." *Chicago Tribune* (Chicago), May 15.

Cameron, Daniel. "Biennial Cycle." *Arts Magazine* (New York), vol. 57, no. 10, June, pp. 64-68.

Glatt, Cara. "Sculptors Look at Human Form." *The Chicago Herald* (Chicago), May 25, p. 10.

Glueck, Grace. "Art: Show Honors de Kooning." *The New York Times* (New York), Dec. 23, p. C22.

Levin, Kim. "Drawings." *The Village Voice* (New York), Aug. 9, p. 56.

Lichtenstein, Therese. "Group Show." *Arts Magazine* (New York), vol. 57, no. 5, Jan., p. 36.

Moser, Charlotte. "Renaissance Show Surveys Ten Years of Using Human Form in Sculpture." *Chicago Sun-Times* (Chicago), May 29, Show section, p.6.

The Renaissance Society at the University of Chicago, Illinois. *The Sixth Day: A Survey of Recent Developments in Figurative Sculpture*, May 8-June 15. Catalogue, text by Richard Flood.

Russell, John. "Art: Show of Drawings at Xavier Fourcade." *The New York Times* (New York), July 29, p. C20.

Westfall, Stephen. "Group Show." *Arts Magazine* (New York), vol. 57, no. 6, Feb., p. 38.

Whitney Museum of American Art, New York. *1983 Biennial Exhibition*, Mar. 24-May 29. Catalogue.

1984
Levin, Kim. "In Honor of de Kooning." *The Village Voice* (New York), Jan. 10, p. 60.

Nancy Dwyer
photograph by Robert Mapplethorpe, March 1983

Nancy Dwyer

Sometimes it seems like rules are made for their own sake, just to give one a reason to make a decision, to think about what is right.

The images were all originally photographs and they come from everywhere common. It seems like I could run out of new pictures, but when I change the channel or turn the page, there's something waiting. It's perfect, but I don't know it until I see it. I'm not searching for the exact image in my mind's eye. The environment is always changing my vision.

I'm moved by idiosyncrasy, particularity and variety over archetype and cliché.

Transferring the picture to line, I attempt control and go public. It's a standard form (a diagram, a cartoon), a processing. The person is a word on a page. Color and form tell the story. This is when time leaves and the rules get lost.

The painting is its own situation. Like a person in this world, it's a forced collaboration of opposing forces. The subjects are humans doing something social. The form is a convention. The environment is hard-edged and abstract with its artificial, contrary coloring. A private morality looks like public domain.

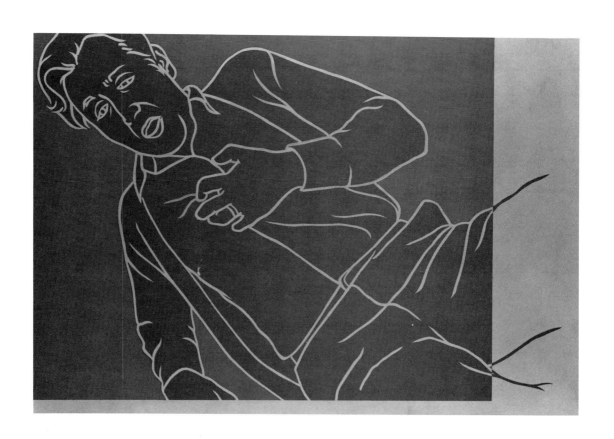

Cholesterol 1982
Acrylic on canvas
48 x 72 in. (121.92 x 182.88 cm.)
Courtesy Semaphore Gallery, New York

Lady Cop 1982
Acrylic on canvas
72 x 48 in. (182.88 x 121.92 cm.)
Courtesy Semaphore Gallery, New York

The Mirror 1983
Acrylic on mirrored Plexiglas and Formica
44¹/₄ x 56 x 3 in. (112.40 x 142.24 x 7.62 cm.)
Courtesy Texas Gallery, Houston

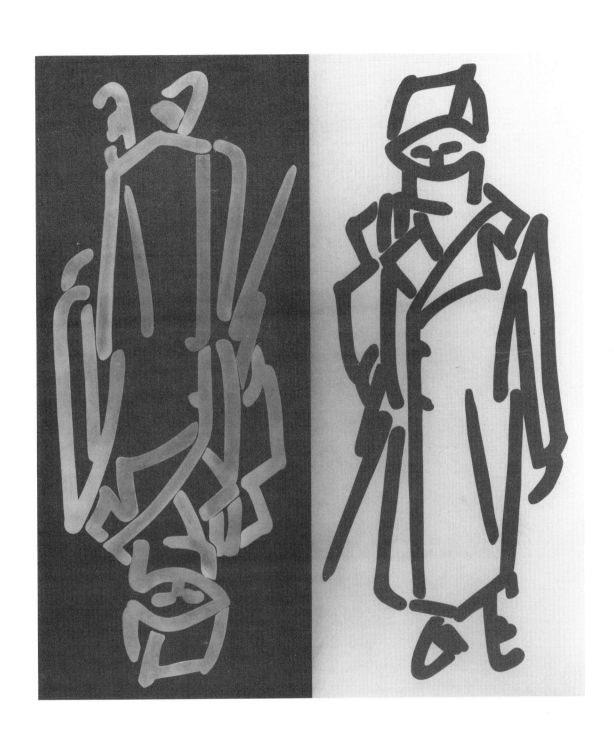

War Boys 1983
Aluminum, Formica and lacquer
62¼ x 55¼ x 5 in. (158.12 x 140.34 x 12.70 cm.)
Courtesy Texas Gallery, Houston

Nancy Dwyer

One-Artist Exhibitions

1977
HALLWALLS, Buffalo, New York.

1980
HALLWALLS, Buffalo, New York.

Artists Space, New York.

1981
Studio d'Arte, Cannaviello, Milan, Italy.

A & M Artworks, New York.

1982
A & M Artworks, New York.

1983
Semaphore Gallery, New York.

Semaphore Gallery, New York.

1984
Texas Gallery, Houston.

Selected Readings

1977
Bannon, Anthony. "The Word on Dwyer: The Writing is on the Wall." *Buffalo Evening News* (Buffalo), Apr. 11, p. 43.

1979
Upton Gallery, State University College, Buffalo, New York. *HALLWALLS: 5 Years*, Nov. 5-15. Catalogue, text by Linda L. Cathcart. Organized by The New Museum, New York. Traveled to A Space, Toronto, Ontario, Canada, Feb. 16-Mar. 8, 1980; Parsons School of Art Gallery, New York, June 20-July 18, 1980.

1980
Ashbery, John. "Art." *New York Magazine* (New York), Oct. 6, p. 63.

Larson, Kay. "Talkin' 'Bout My Generation." *The Village Voice* (New York), June 23, p. 75.

Preisner, Brenda. "Review: Art." *Buffalo Evening News* (Buffalo), Mar. 14, Gusto section, p. 18.

Rickey, Carrie. "Advance to the Rear Guard." *The Village Voice* (New York), Aug. 27, p. 65.

_____. "Babes on West Broadway." *The Village Voice* (New York), July 9, p. 62.

Zimmer, William. "Group Exhibition: Artists Space." *The Soho Weekly News* (New York), Oct. 1-7, p. 81.

1981
Kalil, Susie. "New York Storytellers: Ambiguities and Obfuscations." *Artweek* (Oakland, California), Aug. 11, p. 1.

Parmesani, Loredana. "Nancy Dwyer — Fabio Peloso." *Flash Art* (Milan, Italy), no. 102, Mar.-Apr., p. 48.

Tatransky, Valentin. "Nancy Dwyer." *Arts Magazine* (New York), vol. 55, no. 10, June, p. 4.

1982

Contemporary Arts Center, Cincinnati, Ohio. *Face It: 10 Contemporary Artists*, July 8-Aug. 28. Catalogue, texts by William Olander and Joanna Frueh. Organized by the Ohio Foundation on the Arts. Traveled to The Museums at Hartwick College, Oneonta, New York, Sept. 12-Oct. 16; The College of Wooster Art Museum, Ohio, Oct. 24-Nov. 21; Contemporary Art Center of Cleveland, Ohio, Dec. 3-Jan. 3, 1983; Trisolini Gallery, Ohio University, Athens, Jan. 10-Feb. 12, 1983; University of Colorado Art Galleries, Boulder, Mar. 5-Apr. 9, 1983; Freedman Galleries, Albright College, Reading, Pennsylvania, Mar. 17-June 19, 1983; Doane Hall Art Gallery, Allegheny College, Meadville, Pennsylvania, Oct. 20-Nov. 18, 1983; Southern Ohio Museum and Cultural Center, Portsmouth, Dec. 18, 1983-Jan. 28, 1984.

Goldberg, RoseLee. "Post-TV Art." *Portfolio* (New York), vol. 4, no. 4, July-Aug., pp. 76-79.

Institute of Contemporary Art, University of Pennsylvania, Philadelphia. *Image Scavengers: Painting*, Dec. 8-Jan. 30, 1983. Catalogue, text by Janet Kardon.

The Renaissance Society at the University of Chicago, Illinois. *A Fatal Attraction: Art and the Media*, May 2-June 12. Catalogue, text by Thomas Lawson.

Schoenfeld, Ann. "Paper." *Arts Magazine* (New York), vol. 57, no. 2, Oct., p. 9.

Stapp, Dwayne. "Beast: Animal Imagery." *Arts Magazine* (New York), vol. 57, no. 4, Dec., p. 10.

Tatransky, Valentin. "Three Invited." *Arts Magazine* (New York), vol. 57, no. 1, Sept., pp. 37-38.

1983

Glueck, Grace. "Artists Who 'Scavenge' from the Media." *The New York Times* (New York), Jan. 9, pp. H29-30.

Howell, John. "Art Takes 1: Soho." *New York Beat* (New York), vol. 1, no. 6, Dec., p. 16.

Linker, Kate. "Nancy Dwyer, Semaphore Gallery." *Artforum* (New York), vol. 21, no. 9, May, pp. 99-100.

Smith, Roberta. "Appropriation über Alles." *The Village Voice* (New York), Jan. 11, p. 73.

_____. "Review." *The Village Voice* (New York), Feb. 15, p. 83.

_____. "The Whitney Biennial: Taking Consensus." *The Village Voice* (New York), Apr. 26, pp. 91-92, 108.

1984

Artists Space, New York. *A Decade of New Art*, May 31-June 30. Catalogue, text by Linda L. Cathcart.

Kleyn, Robert. "Protective Mimicry." *Vanguard* (Vancouver, British Columbia, Canada), vol. 13, no. 2, Mar., pp. 25-30.

Krainak, Paul. "Art Comes to Marketplace Rock." *Aquarian Weekly* (New York), no. 521, Apr. 25-May 2, pp. 6-8.

Smith, Roberta. "We Remember MOMA: Temporary Misgivings." *The Village Voice* (New York), May 22, pp. 89, 92.

Whitfield, Tony. "Art Takes." *New York Beat* (New York), vol. 1, no. 11, May, p. 21.

Jedd Garet
photograph by Robert Mapplethorpe, March 1983

Jedd Garet

. . . I look at almost everything. Influences come out of art history, especially clichés of art history. Instead of specific artists, movements are more important to me . . . I don't try to think about a specific painting. When I think about art, I blur the whole thing into a kind of general image. Some of my paintings include a baroque frame; it's not a specific frame, it's just what I remember from every baroque frame I've ever seen. In terms of influences we should include Puerto Rican murals and all other things outside the high art tradition. Wallpaper. Furniture. I love to see what is in this world that has nothing to do with high art . . . .

I don't feel a responsibility to have a vision. I don't think that is quite valid. When I read artists' writings of the past, especially before the two wars, I find it very amusing and I laugh at these things; the spirituality, the changing of the culture. It is possible to change the culture but I don't think art is the right place to try and make an important change except visually, to have people see things differently. I don't consider myself a visionary in the sense that I am going to instruct the culture how to live or how to better themselves because it's a very small world I am dealing with. Art just can't be that world-shattering in this day and age. Not enough people see it. It can filter down, which is ideal, but that takes a long time and goes through too many people. Whatever kind of visual statement you make has to first pass through fashion design and furniture design until it becomes mass-produced; finally, a gas pump might look a little different because of a painting you did. But that's not for the artist to worry about.

Excerpted from Philip Smith, "Jedd Garet and the Atomic Age," *Arts Magazine* (New York), vol. 55, no. 10, June 1981, pp. 158-60.

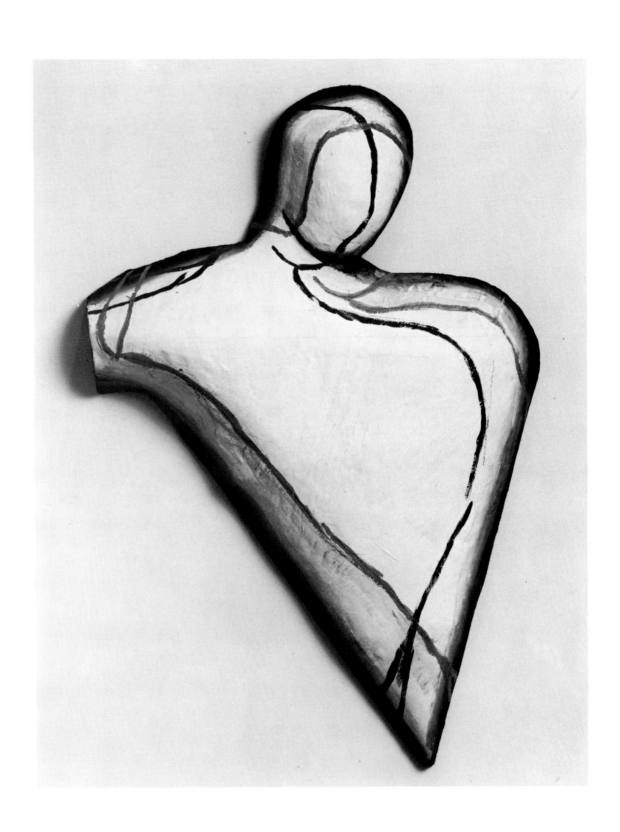

New Servant (Friend and Enemy) 1981
Painted cast aluminum
47 x 32 x 7 in. (119.38 x 81.28 x 17.78 cm.)
Courtesy Texas Gallery, Houston

The Hero of Redworld 1983
Acrylic on canvas
84 x 105 in. (213.36 x 266.70 cm.)
Collection Donald M. Levy M.D., Milwaukee, Wisconsin

Mom and Dad Outside 1983
Acrylic on canvas
95 x 70 x 5 1/2 in. (241.30 x 117.80 x 13.97 cm.)
Collection Mr. and Mrs. Aron B. Katz

54

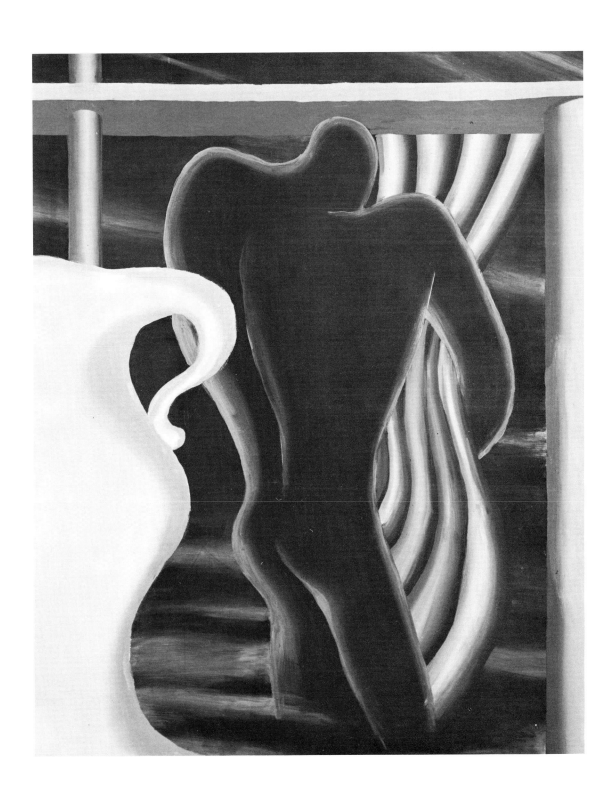

White Vase 1983
Acrylic on canvas
105 x 84 in. (266.70 x 213.36 cm.)
Collection Elaine and Werner Dannheisser

Jedd Garet

One-Artist Exhibitions

1979
Felicity Samuel Gallery, London, England.

Robert Miller Gallery, New York.

1980
Galerie Bruno Bischofberger, Zurich, Switzerland.

1981
Robert Miller Gallery, New York.

HALLWALLS, Buffalo, New York.

Larry Gagosian Gallery, Los Angeles, California.

1982
John Berggruen Gallery, San Francisco, California.

Texas Gallery, Houston.

1983
Robert Miller Gallery, New York.

Michael Lord Gallery, Milwaukee, Wisconsin.

1984
Stephen Wirtz Gallery, San Francisco, California.

Robert Miller Gallery, New York.

Betsy Rosenfield Gallery, Chicago, Illinois.

Selected Readings

1979
Ashbery, John. "Fall Art Previews." *New York Magazine* (New York), Sept. 17, pp. 46-47.

Friedman, Jon. "Jedd Garet." *Arts Magazine* (New York), vol. 54, no. 3, Nov., p. 18.

Kramer, Hilton. "Review." *The New York Times* (New York), Sept. 21, p. C18.

Larson, Kay. "Imperialism with a grain of salt." *The Village Voice* (New York), Sept. 17, p. 79.

Upton Gallery, State University College, Buffalo, New York. *HALLWALLS: 5 Years*, Nov. 5-15. Catalogue, text by Linda L. Cathcart. Organized by The New Museum, New York. Traveled to A Space, Toronto, Ontario, Canada, Feb. 16-Mar. 8, 1980; Parsons School of Art Gallery, New York, June 20-July 18, 1980.

Zimmer, William. "Punky But Oblique." *The Soho Weekly News* (New York), Sept. 20, p. 44.

1980
The Chrysler Museum, Norfolk, Virginia. *American Figure Painting 1950-1980*, Oct. 17-Nov. 30. Catalogue, text by Thomas W. Styron.

1981
Gallati, Barbara. "Jedd Garet." *Arts Magazine* (New York), vol. 55, no. 10, June, pp. 29-30.

HALLWALLS, Buffalo, New York. *Jedd Garet*, Oct. 16-Nov. 17. Catalogue, text by G. Roger Denson.

Henry, Gerrit. "Review." *Art News* (New York), vol. 80, no. 7, Sept., p. 236.

Hughes, Robert. "Quirks, Clamors and Variety." *Time Magazine* (New York), Mar. 2, pp. 84-87.

Knight, Christopher. "Changing Visions Proves Art about Art is not Dead." *Los Angeles Herald Examiner* (Los Angeles), Dec. 20, p. E5.

Levin, Kim. "Jedd Garet: Robert Miller." *Flash Art* (Milan, Italy), no. 103, Summer, p. 54.

Robert Miller Gallery, New York. *Jedd Garet*, Mar. 24-Apr. 11.

Plagens, Peter. "The Academy of the Bad." *Art in America* (New York), vol. 69, no. 9, Nov., pp. 11-17.

Rose, Frank. "Exploring the Art-Rock Nexus (Part II)." *Art Express* (Providence, Rhode Island), vol. 1, no. 3, Nov.-Dec., pp. 39, 43.

Smith, Philip. "Jedd Garet and the Atomic Age." *Arts Magazine* (New York), vol. 55, no. 10, June, pp. 158-60, cover.

Whitney Museum of American Art, New York. *1981 Biennial Exhibition*, Jan. 20-Apr. 19. Catalogue.

1982

Bourdon, David. "The New Expressionists: Battling the Masters: Jedd Garet." *GEO Magazine* (New York), vol. 4, no. 8, Aug., pp. 38-41.

French, P. D. "Disturbing Historical References: Jedd Garet." *Artweek* (Oakland, California), Apr. 17, p. 3.

Hughes, Robert. "Lost Among the Figures." *Time Magazine* (New York), May 31, pp. 64-67.

Hugo, J. "Stylistic Exaggerations: Jedd Garet." *Artweek* (Oakland, California), Jan. 16, p. 2.

Hunter, Sam. "Post-Modernist Painting." *Portfolio* (New York), vol. 4, no. 1, Jan.-Feb., pp. 46-53.

Jan, Alfred. "Double View, Part One: Jedd Garet at John Berggruen." *Images and Issues* (Santa Monica, California), vol. 3, no. 2, Sept.-Oct., pp. 60-61.

Milwaukee Art Museum, Wisconsin. *New Figuration in America*, Dec. 3-Jan. 23, 1983. Catalogue, texts by Russell Bowman and Peter Schjeldahl.

The New Museum, New York. *Extended Sensibilities: Homosexual Presence in Contemporary Art*, Oct. 16-Dec. 30. Catalogue, text by Daniel J. Cameron.

Rickey, Carrie. "Figuratively Speaking." *Art and Auction* (New York), vol. 4, no. 9, June, pp. 36-40.

Singerman, Howard. "Paragraphs Toward An Essay Entitled 'Restoration Comedies'." *Journal* (Los Angeles), no. 33, vol. 4, Summer, pp. 48-51.

Taft, Steven. "Double View, Part Two: Jedd Garet at Larry Gagosian." *Images and Issues* (Santa Monica, California), vol. 3, no. 2, Sept-Oct., p. 61.

University Art Museum, University of California, Santa Barbara. *Figuration*, Jan. 6-Feb. 7. Catalogue, text by Phyllis Plous and Michael R. Klein.

1983

Anderson, Alexander. "Jedd Garet, Robert Miller Gallery." *Flash Art* (Milan, Italy), no. 113, Summer, p. 65.

The Brooklyn Museum, New York. *The American Artist as Printmaker*, Oct. 28-Jan. 22, 1984. Catalogue, text by Barry Walker.

Friedman, Jon R. "Jedd Garet: Robert Miller." *Arts Magazine* (New York), vol. 57, no. 10, June, pp. 32-33.

Gallati, Barbara. "Jedd Garet: Robert Miller." *Arts Magazine* (New York), vol. 57, no. 10, June, pp. 40-41.

Glatt, Cara. "Sculptors look at human form." *The Chicago Herald* (Chicago), May 25, p. 10.

Howe, Katherine. "Landscapes at Robert Miller." *Images and Issues* (Santa Monica, California), vol. 3, no. 4, Jan.-Feb., p. 65.

Larson, Kay. "The New Ugliness." *New York Magazine* (New York), May 30, pp. 64-65.

Moser, Charlotte. "Renaissance show surveys 10 years of using human forms in sculpture." *Chicago Sun-Times* (Chicago), May 29, Show section, p.6.

Nilson, Lisbet. "Making It Neo." *Art News* (New York), vol. 82, no. 7, Sept., pp. 62-70.

The Renaissance Society at the University of Chicago, Illinois. *The Sixth Day: A Survey of Recent Developments in Figurative Sculpture*, May 8-June 15. Catalogue, text by Richard Flood.

1984

Knight, Christopher. "Making Sense of a Decade Full of Artistic Mishmash." *Los Angeles Herald Examiner* (Los Angeles), Apr. 1, p. G11.

Kohn, Michael. "Mannerism and Contemporary Art: The Style and Its Critics." *Arts Magazine* (New York), vol. 57, no. 7, Mar., pp. 72-77.

La Jolla Museum of Contemporary Art, California. *American Art Since 1970*, Mar. 10-Apr. 22. Catalogue, text by Richard Marshall. Organized by the Whitney Museum of American Art, New York. Traveled to Museo Tamayo, Mexico City, Mexico, May 17-July 29; North Carolina Museum of Art, Raleigh, Sept. 29-Nov. 25; Sheldon Memorial Art Gallery, University of Nebraska, Lincoln, Jan. 12-Mar. 3, 1985; Center for the Fine Arts, Miami, Florida, Mar. 30-May 26, 1985.

The Museum of Modern Art, New York. *An International Survey of Recent Painting and Sculpture*, May 17-Aug. 19. Catalogue.

Pincus-Witten, Robert. "Jedd Garet, Nature as Artifice." *Eye to Eye: Twenty Years of Art Criticism*. Ann Arbor: University of Michigan Research Press, pp. 159-68.

San Francisco Museum of Modern Art, California. *The Human Condition: SFMMA Biennial III*, June 28-Aug. 26. Catalogue, texts by Dorothy Martinson, Wolfgang Max Faust, Achille Bonito Oliva, Klaus Ottmann, Edward Kienholz.

Simmons, Chuck. "Blind Swimmer." *Artweek* (Oakland, California), Apr. 28, p. 16.

Wilson, William. "Whitney Spirit Comes to La Jolla." *Los Angeles Times* (Los Angeles), Mar. 25, p. 81.

41st Venice Biennale, Italy. *Paradise Lost/Paradise Regained: American Visions of the New Decade*, June 10-Sept. 30. Catalogue, text by Marcia Tucker.

Thomas Lawson
photograph by Robert Mapplethorpe, March 1983

Thomas Lawson

We gave, fascinated into that fickle mirror which represents (oh, so faithlessly) the best expression of our cherished freedom of speech. We are mesmerized and barely notice as the narcotic slowly leaves us speechless. The chatter continues and the news never stops. Opinion is formed, and we have no part in its forming. Gradually we become little more then eyes, tourists watching the spectacle of our own ruin.

This work is conditioned by a double jeopardy and seeks to locate itself in the dead zone at the center, the zone where meaning quickens or dies. On one side we face the power of the dominant culture to reduce opposition to little more than the gaudy decor of enlightenment. And on the other the insistent penetration of the mass media into every facet of our daily lives has made the chance of authentic experience difficult, if not impossible.

"Every cigarette, every drink, every love affair echoes down a never-ending passageway of references — to advertisements, to the television shows, to movies, to headlines — to the point we no longer know if we mimic or are mimicked. We flicker around the flame of our desire, loving the comfort of repeating a well-worn language and its well-worn sentiments, fearful of losing all control to that language and the society it represents, uncertain of how to resist. We are trapped firmly within the terms of a fatal attraction, driven to say "no," unable to say it with any conviction."[1]

[1] Thomas Lawson, "A Fatal Attraction," *A Fatal Attraction: Art and the Media* (exhibition catalogue), (Chicago: The Renaissance Society, 1982), p. 3.

Battered to Death 1981
Oil on canvas
48 x 48 in. (121.92 x 121.92 cm.)
Courtesy Metro Pictures, New York

Boy Shot for Bike 1981
Oil on canvas
48 x 48 in. (121.92 x 121.92 cm.)
Courtesy Metro Pictures, New York

61

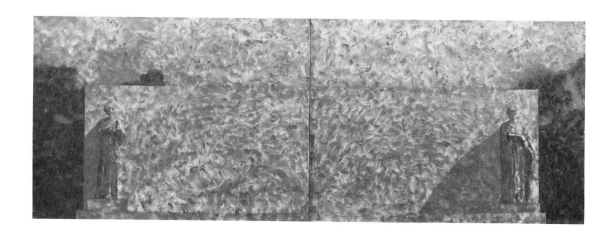

Saved 1982
Oil on canvas
48 x 96 in. (121.92 x 243.84 cm.)
Courtesy Metro Pictures, New York

To Those Who Follow After 1983
Oil on canvas
60 x 168 in. (152.40 x 426.72 cm.)
Courtesy Metro Pictures, New York

Thomas Lawson

One-Artist Exhibitions

1976
Pleiades, New York.

1977
Artists Space, New York.

18th Floor Gallery, City University of New York, Graduate Center, New York.

1980
Mercer Union Front Gallery, Toronto, Ontario, Canada.

1981
Metro Pictures, New York.

1982
Metro Pictures, New York.

1983
Metro Pictures, New York.

Richard Kuhlenschmidt Gallery, Los Angeles, California.

Selected Readings

1976
Amen, Grover. "Tom Lawson at Pleiades." *Arts Magazine* (New York), vol. 51, no. 2, Oct., pp. 29-30.

Betz, Margaret. "Tom Lawson at Pleiades." *Art News* (New York), vol. 75, no. 8, Oct., p. 126.

1978
Ashbery, John. "Yule Log." *New York Magazine* (New York), Dec. 25, p. 92.

1979
Lawson, Thomas. "The Uses of Representation: Making Some Distinctions." *Flash Art* (Milan, Italy), no. 88-89, Mar.-Apr., pp. 37-39.

Tatransky, Valentin. "Four Scottish Artists, Artists Space." *Arts Magazine* (New York), vol. 53, no. 10, June, p. 36.

1980
Brooke Alexander Inc., New York. *Illustration & Allegory*, May 13-June 14. Catalogue, text by Carter Ratcliff.

Oliva, Achille Bonito. "The Bewildered Image." *Flash Art* (Milan, Italy), no. 96 -97, Mar.-Apr., pp. 32-41.

Phillips, Deborah C. "Illustration & Allegory, Brooke Alexander." *Arts Magazine* (New York), vol. 55, no. 1, Sept., pp. 25-26.

Rickey, Carrie. "Naive Nouveau and Its Malcontents." *Flash Art* (Milan, Italy), no. 98-99, Summer, pp. 36-39.

Simon, Joan. "Double Takes." *Art in America* (New York), vol. 68, no. 8, Oct., pp. 113-17.

Tatransky, Valentin. "Illustration & Allegory." *Arts Magazine* (New York), vol. 55, no. 1, Sept., p. 4.

1981
Casademont, Joan. "Thomas Lawson: Metro Pictures." *Artforum* (New York), vol. 20, no. 1, Sept., p. 74.

HALLWALLS, Buffalo, New York. *Figuring*, Mar. 6-31. Catalogue, text by Valentin Tatransky.

Lawson, Thomas. "Too Good to be True." *Real Life Magazine* (New York), no. 7, Autumn, p. 4.

Tatransky, Valentin. "Eric Fischl, Thomas Lawson, Walter Robinson and David Sharpe." *Flash Art* (Milan, Italy), no. 103, Summer, pp. 42-43.

_____. "Fischl, Lawson, Robinson, and Zwack: they make pictures." *Arts Magazine* (New York), vol. 55, no. 10, June, pp. 147-49.

1982
Donahue, Geralyn and Wallace, Joan. "The Difference Between Absence and Not Being Missed." *Journal* (Los Angeles), no. 33, vol. 4, Summer, pp. 38-41.

Foster, Hal. "Between Modernism and the Media." *Art in America* (New York), vol. 70, no. 7, Summer, pp. 13-17.

Institute of Contemporary Art, University of Pennsylvania, Philadelphia. *Image Scavengers: Painting*, Dec. 8-Jan. 30, 1983. Catalogue, text by Janet Kardon.

Kuspit, Donald B. "Critical Perspectives at P.S.1." *Artforum* (New York), vol. 20, no. 8, Apr., pp. 81-83.

_____. "Thomas Lawson: Metro Pictures." *Artforum* (New York), vol. 20, no. 9, May, pp. 83-84.

Lawson, Thomas. "The Dark Side of the Bright Light." *Artforum* (New York), vol. 21, no. 3, Nov., pp. 62-66.

_____ and an interview with the artist by Kate Horsfield. "Thomas Lawson." *Profile* (Chicago), vol. 4, no. 2, Mar.

Linker, Kate. "Melodramatic Tactics." *Artforum* (New York), vol. 21, no. 1, Sept., pp. 30-32.

Milwaukee Art Museum, Wisconsin. *New Figuration in America*, Dec. 3-Jan. 23, 1983. Catalogue, texts by Russell Bowman and Peter Schjeldahl.

Moufarrege, Nicolas A. "The Erotic Impulse." *Arts Magazine* (New York), vol. 57, no. 3, Nov., p. 5.

Ratcliff, Carter. "Art & Resentment." *Art in America* (New York), vol. 70, no. 7, Summer, pp. 9-13.

The Renaissance Society at the University of Chicago, Illinois. *A Fatal Attraction: Art and the Media*, May 2-June 12. Catalogue, text by Thomas Lawson.

Schjeldahl, Peter. "Mind over Matter." *The Village Voice* (New York), Mar. 9, p. 79.

Singerman, Howard. "Paragraphs Toward an Essay Entitled 'Restoration Comedies'." *Journal* (Los Angeles), no. 33, vol. 4, Summer, pp. 48-51.

Smith, Roberta. "Surface Values." *The Village Voice* (New York), Apr. 13, p. 80.

Smith, Valerie. "Painting: Metro Pictures." *Flash Art* (Milan, Italy), no. 107, May, p. 49.

Whitney Museum of American Art, Downtown Branch, New York. *Frames of Reference*, May 6-June 4. Catalogue, text by Nora Halpern.

1983
Armstrong, Richard. "Other Views." *Artforum* (New York), vol. 22, no. 4, Dec., p. 83.

Brenson, Michael. "Thomas Lawson." *The New York Times* (New York), Dec. 16, p. C30.

Glueck, Grace. "Artists Who 'Scavenge' from the Media." *The New York Times* (New York), Jan. 9, pp. H29-30.

Hicks, Emily. "Stories About Painting." *Artweek* (Oakland, California), Nov. 12, p. 6.

Howell, John. "Art Takes 1: Soho." *New York Beat* (New York), vol. 1, no. 6, Dec., p. 16.

Kirshner, Judith Russi. "Compassionate Images, N.A.M.E. Gallery." *Artforum* (New York), vol. 21, no. 9, May, pp. 102-03.

Rhodes, Richard. "Real Lives." *Vanguard* (Vancouver, British Columbia, Canada), vol. 12, no. 1, Feb., pp. 19-22.

Robbins, David A. "An Interview with Thomas Lawson." *Arts Magazine* (New York), vol. 58, no. 1, Sept., pp. 114-17, cover.

Rooney, Robert. "Interview with Thomas Lawson." *Art & Text* (South Yarra, Victoria, Australia), Summer, pp. 38-47.

Schjeldahl, Peter. "Falling in Style, The New Art and Our Discontents." *Vanity Fair* (New York), vol. 46, no. 1, Mar., pp. 115-17.

Smith, Roberta. "Appropriation über Alles." *The Village Voice* (New York), Jan. 11, p. 73.

Starenko, Michael. "What's An Artist to Do? A Short History of Postmodernism and Photography." *Afterimage* (New York), vol. 10, no. 6, Jan., pp. 4-5.

Tatransky, Valentin. "Group Show." *Arts Magazine* (New York), vol. 57, no. 7, Mar., p. 16.

1984
Artists Space, New York. *A Decade of New Art*, May 31-June 30. Catalogue, text by Linda L. Cathcart.

H[eartney], E[leanor]. "Thomas Lawson: Metro Pictures." *Art News* (New York), vol. 83, no. 3, Mar., p. 215.

Levin, Kim. "Thomas Lawson." *The Village Voice* (New York), Jan. 10, p. 60.

Liebmann, Lisa. "Thomas Lawson, Metro Pictures." *Artforum* (New York), vol. 22, no. 7, Mar., pp. 95-96.

Robert Longo
photograph by Robert Mapplethorpe, March 1983

Robert Longo

. . . the other day I was sitting here at my table, I had a Vogue *magazine open in front of me,
a* Newsweek *to my left, I was watching TV, I was looking at some Polaroids and I was making a drawing. And I realized I live totally in a world of "representation." I think of myself as "the new astronaut,"
in a new frontier, I live in a boundless universe . . . . My sense of reality is that there is none. I never
have time to be in reality because I am constantly making a reality . . . being an American seems critical at this time. It's not something I go out to portray, rather it is a consequence I have to carry . . . I
think often about freedom . . . . In my art I am trying to deal with something like the nature of being condemned . . . . I don't have to be delicate about art history or pop imagery, I smash them together and
stand back and see what happens . . . . I'm carrying on experiments with images and testing them on
the viewer . . . I want to instigate something.*

Culture Culture 1982-83
Mixed media
91 1/2 x 147 3/4 in. (232.41 x 375.29 cm.)
Collection the artist
Courtesy Metro Pictures, New York

V 1983-84
Mixed media
129¹/₂ x 114 x 36 in. (328.93 x 289.56 x 91.44 cm.)
Private Collection
Courtesy Metro Pictures, New York

Robert Longo

One-Artist Exhibitions and Performances
1974
Gallery 220, State University College, Buffalo, New York.

Upton Gallery, State University College, Buffalo, New York.

1976
Visual Studies Workshop, Rochester, New York.

Vehicule Art, Montreal, Quebec, Canada.

HALLWALLS, Buffalo, New York.

1977
The Kitchen, New York.

Artists Space, New York (Performance and Installation).

1978
Franklin Furnace, New York (Performance).

1979
The Kitchen, New York (Performance).

1980
Studio d'Arte, Cannaviello, Milan, Italy.

Moderna Museet, Stockholm, Sweden (Performance). Circulated.

1981
Metro Pictures, New York.

Fine Arts Center, University of Rhode Island, Kingston.

Larry Gagosian Gallery, Los Angeles, California.

The Corcoran Gallery of Art, Washington, D.C. (Performance).

Real Art Ways, University of Hartford, Connecticut.

1982
Texas Gallery, Houston.

The Kitchen, New York (Performance).

1983
Brooke Alexander Inc., New York.

Leo Castelli Gallery and Metro Pictures, New York.

Galerie Schellmann & Kluser, Munich, West Germany.

1984
Akron Art Museum, Ohio.

Metro Pictures, New York.

Selected Readings
1977
Albright-Knox Art Gallery, Buffalo, New York. *In Western New York*, Mar. 26-Apr. 17. Catalogue.

Artists Space, New York. *Pictures*, Sept. 24-Oct. 29. Catalogue, text by Douglas Crimp.

Zimmer, William. "Pictures and Statements." *The Soho Weekly News* (New York), Oct. 6-12.

1978
Frank, Peter. "Pictures and Meaning." *Artweek* (Oakland, California), Apr. 29, p. 5.

Henry, Gerrit. "Pictures." *Art News* (New York), vol. 77, no. 1, Jan., pp. 142-43.

Lawson, Thomas. "'Pictures' at Artists Space." *Art in America* (New York), vol. 66, no. 1, Jan.-Feb., p. 118.

1979
Cathcart, Linda L. "The Western Image in New York: Longo, Sherman, Zwack." *Arts Quarterly* (New Orleans), no. 1, Oct.-Nov.-Dec., pp. 8-9.

Crimp, Douglas. "Pictures." *October* (Cambridge, Massachusetts), no. 8, Spring, pp. 75-88.

Fox, Howard. "Desire for Pathos: The Art of Robert Longo." *Sun & Moon* (College Park, Maryland), no. 8, Fall, pp. 71-80.

Goldberg, RoseLee. *Performance: Live Art, 1909 to the Present*. New York: Harry N. Abrams, Inc., p. 122.

Lawson, Thomas. "The Uses of Representation: Making Some Distinctions." *Flash Art* (Milan, Italy), no. 88-89, Mar.-Apr., pp. 37-39.

Upton Gallery, State University College, Buffalo, New York. *HALLWALLS: 5 Years*, Nov. 5-15. Catalogue, text by Linda L. Cathcart. Organized by The New Museum, New York. Traveled to A Space, Toronto, Ontario, Canada, Feb. 16-Mar. 8, 1980; Parsons School of Art Gallery, New York, June 20-July 18, 1980.

1980
Brooke Alexander Inc., New York. *Illustration & Allegory*, May 13-June 14. Catalogue, text by Carter Ratcliff.

Contemporary Arts Museum, Houston, Texas. *Extensions: Jennifer Bartlett, Lynda Benglis, Robert Longo, Judy Pfaff*, Jan. 19-Mar. 2. Catalogue, text by Linda L. Cathcart.

Crossley, Mimi. "Review: Extensions." *The Houston Post* (Houston), Jan. 25, pp. 1E, 5E.

Goldberg, RoseLee. "Performance-Art for All." *Art Journal* (New York), vol. 40, no. 1-2, Fall-Winter, p. 375.

Kalil, Susie. "Issues in Extension: Contemporary Arts Museum, Houston, Texas." *Artweek* (Oakland, California), Feb. 9, p. 1.

Owens, Craig. "The Allegorical Impulse: toward a theory of postmodernism, parts I and II." *October* (Cambridge, Massachusetts), vol. 12; 13, Spring; Summer, pp. 67-86; 59-80.

Rickey, Carrie. "Naive Nouveau and Its Malcontents." *Flash Art* (Milan, Italy), no. 98-99, Summer, pp. 36-39.

Shore, Michael. "How Does It Look? How Does It Sound?" *Art News* (New York), vol. 79, no. 9, Nov., pp. 78-85.

Siegel, Jeanne. "Lois Lane and Robert Longo: Interpretation of Image." *Arts Magazine* (New York), vol. 55, no. 3, Nov., pp. 154-57.

Simon, Joan. "Double Takes." *Art in America* (New York), vol. 68, no. 8, Oct., pp. 113-17.

Tennant, Donna. "Four Artists Struggle for Originality." *Houston Chronicle* (Houston), Jan. 27, pp. 15, 29.

1981
Albright-Knox Art Gallery, CEPA Gallery and HALLWALLS, Buffalo, New York. *Figures: Forms and Expressions*, Nov. 21-Jan. 3, 1982. Catalogue, texts by G. Roger Denson, Biff Henrich, Charlotta Kotik and Susan Krane.

Atkins, Robert. "Robert Longo at the Corcoran Art School." *Images and Issues* (Santa Monica, California), vol. 2, no. 2, Fall, pp. 74-75.

Blinderman, Barry. "Robert Longo's 'Men in the Cities:' Quotes and Commentary." *Arts Magazine* (New York), vol. 55, no. 7, Mar., pp. 92-93, cover.

Casademont, Joan. "Represent, Representation, Representative." *Artforum* (New York), vol. 20, no. 4, Dec., pp. 73-74.

Crimp, Douglas. "The Photographic Activity of Postmodernism." *October* (Cambridge, Massachusetts), no. 15, Winter, pp. 91-101.

Hayden Gallery, Massachusetts Institute of Technology, Cambridge. *Body Language: Figurative Aspects of Recent Art*, Oct. 2-Dec. 24. Catalogue, text by Roberta Smith. Traveled to The Fort Worth Art Museum, Texas, Sept. 11-Oct. 24, 1982; University of South Florida Art Gallery, Tampa, Nov. 12-Dec. 17, 1982; Contemporary Arts Center, Cincinnati, Ohio, Jan. 13-Feb. 27, 1983.

Hicks, Emily. "Death in the Age of Mechanical Reproduction: Robert Longo." *Artweek* (Oakland, California), July 4, p. 4.

Larson, Kay. "Sculpting Figuratively." *New York Magazine* (New York), Nov. 16, p. 120.

Levin, Kim. "Robert Longo, Metro Pictures." *Flash Art* (Milan, Italy), no. 102, Mar.-Apr., p. 40.

Marzorati, Gerald. "Monumental Confrontations: Guerilla Proposals for Real Public Art." *The Soho Weekly News* (New York), Apr. 8-14.

Nadelman, Cynthia. "New York Reviews: Robert Longo (Metro Pictures)." *Art News* (New York), vol. 80, no. 4, Apr., p. 194.

Owens, Craig. "Robert Longo at Metro Pictures." *Art in America* (New York), vol. 69, no. 3, Mar., pp. 125-26.

Ratcliff, Carter. "Art Stars for the Eighties." *Saturday Review* (New York), vol. 8, Feb., pp. 12-15, 20.

_____. "Westkunst: Robert Longo." *Flash Art* (Milan, Italy), no. 103, Summer, pp. 30-31.

Wave Hill, Bronx, New York. *Tableaux*, May 15-Oct. 13. Catalogue, text by Kim Levin.

Wohlfert, Lee. "New York's Young Sculptors." *Town and Country* (New York), vol. 135, no. 5017, Sept., pp. 259, 261, 263-64, 266.

Zimmer, William. "Robert Longo: Metro Pictures." *The Soho Weekly News* (New York), Jan. 21-27.

1982

Banes, Sally. "Performance: The Long and Short of It." *The Village Voice* (New York), May 18, p. 88.

Goldberg, RoseLee. "Post-TV Art." *Portfolio* (New York), vol. 4, no. 4, July-Aug., pp. 76-79.

Hughes, Robert. "Lost Among the Figures." *Time Magazine* (New York), May 31, pp. 64-67.

Hutton, John. "The Anxious Figure." *Arts Magazine* (New York), vol. 56, no. 5, Jan., p. 17.

Institute of Contemporary Art, University of Pennsylvania, Philadelphia. *Image Scavengers: Painting*, Dec. 8-Jan. 30, 1983. Catalogue, text by Janet Kardon.

Kontova, Helena. "From Performance to Painting." *Flash Art* (Milan, Italy), no. 106, Feb.-Mar., pp. 16-21.

Longo, Robert. "Empire: A Performance Trilogy." *Wedge* (New York), no. 1, Summer, pp. 66-71.

Milwaukee Art Museum, Wisconsin. *New Figuration in America*, Dec. 3-Jan. 23, 1983. Catalogue, texts by Russell Bowman and Peter Schjeldahl.

Pincus-Witten, Robert. "Defenestrations: Robert Longo and Ross Bleckner." *Arts Magazine* (New York), vol. 57, no. 3, Nov., pp. 94-95.

Ratcliff, Carter. "Contemporary American Art." *Flash Art* (Milan, Italy), no. 108, Summer, pp. 32-35.

The Renaissance Society at the University of Chicago, Illinois. *A Fatal Attraction: Art and the Media*, May 2-June 12. Catalogue, text by Thomas Lawson.

Roberts, John. "The Art of Self-Attention." *Artscribe* (London, England), no. 36, Aug., pp. 50-55.

Siegel, Jeanne. "The New Reliefs." *Arts Magazine* (New York), vol. 56, no. 8, Apr., pp. 140-44.

Walker Art Center, Minneapolis, Minnesota. *Eight Artists: The Anxious Edge*, Apr. 25-June 13. Catalogue, text by Lisa Lyons.

Wallis, Brian. "Governing Authority: Robert Longo's Performance Empire." *Wedge* (New York), no. 1, Summer, pp. 64-65.

Whitney Museum of American Art, New York. *Focus on the Figure: Twenty Years*, Apr. 14-June 13. Catalogue, text by Barbara Haskell.

Whitney Museum of American Art, Downtown Branch, New York. *Frames of Reference*, May 6-June 4. Catalogue, text by Nora Halpern.

1983

Artner, Alan G. "The return of the human touch: Figurative sculpture is really back in vogue." *Chicago Tribune* (Chicago), May 15.

Ashbery, John. "Biennials Bloom in the Spring." *Newsweek* (New York), Apr. 18, pp. 93-94.

Brooks, Rosetta. "Robert Longo, Leo Castelli Gallery and Metro Pictures." *Artforum* (New York), vol. 21, no. 10, June, pp. 83-84.

Ciardi, Nives. "Robert Longo." *Domus* (Milan, Italy), no. 635, Jan., p. 69.

Collins, Tricia and Milazzo, Robert. "Robert Longo: Static Violence." *Flash Art* (Milan, Italy), no. 112, May, pp. 36-38.

Eisenman, Stephen F. "Robert Longo: Leo Castelli, Metro Pictures." *Arts Magazine* (New York), vol. 57, no. 8, Apr., p. 43.

Foster, Hal. "The Art of Spectacle." *Art in America* (New York), vol. 71, no. 4, Apr., pp. 144-49, 195, 197, 199.

Glatt, Cara. "Sculptors look at human form." *The Chicago Herald* (Chicago), May 25, p. 10.

Glueck, Grace. "Artists Who 'Scavenge' from the Media." *The New York Times* (New York), Jan. 9, pp. H29-30.

_____. "Big American Figure Drawings." *The New York Times* (New York), Mar. 18, p. C23.

_____. "Art: Works by Longo On View at Two Galleries." *The New York Times* (New York), Feb. 11, p. C22.

Hirshhorn Museum and Sculpture Garden, Washington, D.C. *Directions 1983*, Mar. 10-May 15. Catalogue, text by Phyllis D. Rosenzweig.

Hughes, Robert. "Three From The Image Machine." *Time Magazine* (New York), Mar. 14, pp. 83-84.

Kuspit, Donald B. "New Figuration in America at the Milwaukee Art Museum." *Art in America* (New York), vol. 71, no. 8, Sept., pp. 178-79.

Moser, Charlotte. "Renaissance show surveys 10 years of using human forms in sculpture." *Chicago Sun-Times* (Chicago), May 29, Show section, p.6.

Nilson, Lisbet. "Making It Neo." *Art News* (New York), vol. 82, no. 7, Sept., pp. 62-70.

Ratcliff, Carter. "Robert Longo." *Interview* (New York), vol. 23, no. 4, Apr., pp. 78-81.

The Renaissance Society at the University of Chicago, Illinois. *The Sixth Day: A Survey of Recent Developments in Figurative Sculpture*, May 8-June 15. Catalogue, text by Richard Flood.

Schjeldahl, Peter. "Falling in Style, The New Art and Our Discontents." *Vanity Fair* (New York), vol. 46, no. 1, Mar., pp. 115-17.

_____. "Vanity Fair Notes: Robert Longo." *Vanity Fair* (New York), vol. 46, no. 3, May.

Smith, Roberta. "Appropriation über Alles." *The Village Voice* (New York), Jan. 11, p. 73.

_____. "Making Impressions." *The Village Voice* (New York), Mar. 1, p. 79.

Weisberg, Ruth. "Representational Drawing: The Power of Subjectivity." *Artweek* (Oakland, California), Apr. 2, p. 1.

Whitney Museum of American Art, New York. *1983 Biennial Exhibition*, Mar. 15-May 22. Catalogue.

Wintour, Anna. "Fall Fashion: Painting the Town." *New York Magazine* (New York), Aug. 29, pp. 54, cover.

Zelevansky, Lynn. "Robert Longo: Leo Castelli, Metro Pictures." *Art News* (New York), vol. 82, no. 4, Apr., p. 152.

1984

Akron Art Museum, Ohio. *Robert Longo: Drawings & Reliefs*, Apr. 7-June 10. Catalogue, text by Hal Foster.

Artists Space, New York. *A Decade of New Art*, May 31-June 30. Catalogue, text by Linda L. Cathcart.

Battcock, Gregory and Nickas, Robert. *The Art of Performance: A Critical Anthology*. New York: E.P. Dutton, Inc., pp. 36, 71, 73, 89, 91.

Brenson, Michael. "Art: Apocalyptic Pop in Mixed-Media Show." *The New York Times* (New York), May 4, p. C26.

Goldberg, RoseLee. "Robert Longo's Solid Vision." *New York Beat* (New York), vol. 1, no. 11, May, pp. 8-9, cover.

Longo, Robert. "Robert Longo Talking About *The Sword of the Pig*." London, England: Tate Gallery.

The Museum of Modern Art, New York. *An International Survey of Recent Painting and Sculpture*, May 17-Aug. 19. Catalogue.

Pincus-Witten, Robert. "Entries: Propaedeutica." *Arts Magazine* (New York), vol. 58, no. 7, Mar., p. 96.

San Francisco Museum of Modern Art, California. *The Human Condition: SFMMA Biennial III*, June 28-Aug. 26. Catalogue, texts by Dorothy Martinson, Wolfgang Max Faust, Achille Bonito Oliva, Klaus Ottmann, Edward Kienholz.

Smith, Roberta. "Material Concerns." *The Village Voice* (New York), May 29, p. 85.

Robert Mapplethorpe
photograph by Robert Mapplethorpe, March 1983

Robert Mapplethorpe

. . . What makes my pictures different from somebody else's? I think the important part is to somehow connect with the model, the subject in the photograph. That's not necessarily done in the studio. I always show pictures so that people can see where I'm coming from, so they can see how I relate to what I'm doing. The secret of it all is to have a kind of personal rapport with the subject that isn't like anybody else's.

. . . I think the flowers have this edge to them — I don't know what it is exactly because I'm just using daylight. But there is a certain edge. I don't know if nasty is the right word — if you look at that picture of the orchid, to me it's a kind of scorpion — it has a sharpness to it. It's composition. I think there is a definite consistency from one subject to another. If I photograph a flower or a cock, I'm not doing anything different, I'm just zeroing in on a different subject. With the flower the only difference is that it's a still-life and I don't have to worry about long exposure. I can work a little bit more on composition than if I were working with a model.

Excerpted from an interview with Robert Mapplethorpe by Robert Hayes in *Interview* (New York). vol. 13. no. 3. Mar. 1983. pp. 50-54.

Eighteen Photographs 1982-83 (detail)
Gelatin silver prints
18 photographs: each 20 x 16 in.
(50.80 x 40.64 cm.)
Courtesy Robert Miller Gallery, New York

Glenn Close 1982
Gelatin silver print
20 x 16 in. (50.80 x 40.64 cm.)
Courtesy Robert Miller Gallery, New York

Donald Sutherland 1983
Gelatin silver print
20 x 16 in. (50.80 x 40.64 cm.)
Courtesy Robert Miller Gallery, New York

Ed Ruscha 1984
Gelatin silver print
20 x 16 in. (50.80 x 40.64 cm.)
Courtesy Robert Miller Gallery, New York

Ellen Barkin 1984
Gelatin silver print
20 x 16 in. (50.80 x 40.64 cm.)
Courtesy Robert Miller Gallery, New York

Ellsworth Kelly 1984
Gelatin silver print
20 x 16 in. (50.80 x 40.64 cm.)
Courtesy Robert Miller Gallery, New York

Robert Mapplethorpe

One-Artist Exhibitions
1976
Light Gallery, New York.
1977
Holly Solomon Gallery, New York.

The Kitchen, New York.

Holly Solomon Gallery, New York.
1978
La Remise du Parc Gallery, Paris, France.

Robert Miller Gallery, New York.

The Chrysler Museum, Norfolk, Virginia.

Langdon Street Gallery, San Francisco, California.

Simon Lowinsky Gallery, San Francisco, California.

The Corcoran Gallery of Art, Washington, D.C.

Los Angeles Institute of Contemporary Art, Los Angeles, California.
1979
Robert Samuel Gallery, New York.

Texas Gallery, Houston.

Robert Miller Gallery, New York.

International Center of Photography, New York.

1980
Vision Gallery, Boston, Massachusetts.

Galerie Jurka, Amsterdam, The Netherlands.

Lawson/De Celle Gallery, Los Angeles, California.

In a Plain Brown Wrapper Gallery, Chicago, Illinois.

Stuart Gallery, Chicago, Illinois.

Contretype Espace Photographique, Brussels, Belgium.

Van Reekum Museum, Apeldoom, The Netherlands.
1981
Fraenkel Gallery, San Francisco, California.

Lunn Gallery, Washington, D.C.

Galerie Texbraun, Paris, France.

Robert Miller Gallery, New York.

Frankfurter Kunstverein, Frankfurt, West Germany.

Galerie Nagel, West Berlin, West Germany.

Contretype Espace Photographique, Brussels, Belgium.

ACE Gallery, Los Angeles, California.
1982
Galleria Il Ponte, Rome, Italy.

Galerie Ton Peek, Utrecht, The Netherlands.

Fay Gold Gallery, Atlanta, Georgia.

Young/Hoffman Gallery, Chicago, Illinois.

Larry Gagosian Gallery, Los Angeles, California.

Shore Gallery, The Pines, Long Island, New York.

Galerie Jurka, Amsterdam, The Netherlands.

Contemporary Arts Center, New Orleans, Louisiana.

Fraenkel Gallery, San Francisco, California.

1983
Robert Miller Gallery, New York.

Sam Hardison Fine Arts Ltd., New York.

Leo Castelli Gallery, New York.

Jane Corkin Gallery, Toronto, Ontario, Canada.

Centre Georges Pompidou, Paris, France.

Rudigar Schottle Gallery, Munich, West Germany.

Photografie Gallery, Dusseldorf, West Germany.

Olympus Centre, London, England.

Galerie Watari, Tokyo, Japan.

Institute of Contemporary Arts, London, England. Circulated.

St. Louis Art Museum, Missouri.

Barbara Gladstone Gallery, New York.
1984
Palazzo Fortuny, Venice, Italy. Circulated.

Galeria Fernando Vijande, Madrid, Spain.

Lucio Amelio Foundation, Naples, Italy.

Selected Readings
1977
Bourdon, David. "Robert Mapplethorpe." *Arts Magazine* (New York), vol. 51, no. 8, Apr., p. 7.

Henry, Gerrit. "Outlandish nature." *Art News* (New York), vol. 76, no. 4, Apr., p. 118.

Tatransky, Valentin. "Robert Mapplethorpe: Holly Solomon." *Arts Magazine* (New York), vol. 51, no. 9, May, p. 29.

"Transfiguration/configuration: Mapplethorpe." *Camera* (Philadelphia, Pennsylvania), vol. 56, Summer, pp. 4-13.

1978
The Chrysler Museum, Norfolk, Virginia. *Robert Mapplethorpe Photographs*, Jan. 18-Mar. 12. Catalogue.

Creatis (Paris, France), no. 7. Issue devoted to the work of Robert Mapplethorpe.

Foster, Hal. "Robert Mapplethorpe, Holly Solomon Gallery." *Artforum* (New York), vol. 16, no. 6, Feb., pp. 68-69.

1979
Friedman, Jon R. "Robert Mapplethorpe: Robert Miller Gallery." *Arts Magazine* (New York), vol. 53, no. 10, June, p. 32.

Galerie Jurka, Amsterdam, The Netherlands. *Robert Mapplethorpe*, Apr. Catalogue.

Lifson, Ben. "The Philistine Photographer: Reassessing Mapplethorpe." *The Village Voice* (New York), Apr. 9, p. 79.

Perrone, Jeff. "Robert Mapplethorpe: Robert Miller Gallery." *Artforum* (New York), vol. 17, no. 10, Summer, pp. 70-71.

1980
Galerie Jurka, Amsterdam, The Netherlands. *Black Males by Robert Mapplethorpe*, Nov. Catalogue, text by Edmund White.

1981
Albright-Knox Art Gallery, CEPA Gallery and HALLWALLS, Buffalo, New York. *Figures: Forms and Expressions*, Nov. 20-Jan.3, 1982. Catalogue, text by G. Roger Denson, Biff Henrich, Charlotta Kotik and Susan Krane.

Ellenzweig, Allen. "Robert Mapplethorpe at Robert Miller." *Art in America* (New York), vol. 69, no. 9, Nov., pp. 171-72.

Fischer, H. "Calculated Opulence." *Artweek* (Oakland, California), Nov. 21, p. 11.

Flood, Richard. "Skied and Grounded in Queens 'New York/New Wave' at P.S. 1." *Artforum* (New York), vol. 19, no. 10, June, pp. 84-87.

Frankfurter Kunstverein, Frankfurt, West Germany. *Robert Mapplethorpe*, Apr. 10-May 17. Catalogue, text by Sam Wagstaff.

Hershkovitz, David. "Shock of the Black and the Blue." *The Soho Weekly News* (New York), May 20-26, pp. 9-11.

Whitney Museum of American Art, New York. *1981 Biennial Exhibition*, Jan. 20-Apr. 19. Catalogue.

1982
Henry, Gerrit. "Robert Mapplethorpe— Collecting Quality: An Interview." *The Print Collector's Newsletter* (New York), vol. 13, no. 4, Sept.-Oct., pp. 128-30.

Kohn, Michael. "Robert Mapplethorpe: Larry Gagosian." *Arts Magazine* (New York), vol. 57, no. 1, Sept., p. 43.

Levy, Mark. "Robert Mapplethorpe at Fraenkel Gallery." *Images and Issues* (Santa Monica, California), vol. 2, no. 4, Spring, pp. 77-78.

Muchnic, Suzanne. "Galleries." *Los Angeles Times* (Los Angeles), July 9, p. 11.

Pousner, Howard. "Shoot first, ask questions later." *The Atlanta Journal* (Atlanta), Apr. 17.

1983
Chatwin, Bruce. *Lady: Lisa Lyon by Robert Mapplethorpe*. New York: Viking Press.

Grundberg, Andy. "Is Mapplethorpe Only Out to Shock?" *The New York Times* (New York), Mar. 13, pp. 32, 35.

Hayes, Robert. "Interview with Robert Mapplethorpe." *Interview* (New York), vol. 13, no. 3, Mar., pp. 50-54.

Himmel, Eric. "Cut Flowers." *Camera Arts* (New York), vol. 3, no. 4, Apr., pp. 56-61.

Institute of Contemporary Arts, London, England. *Robert Mapplethorpe 1970-1983*, Nov. 4-Dec. 18. Catalogue, texts by Stuart Morgan and Alan Hollinghurst. Traveled to Stills, Edinburgh, Scotland, Aug. 19-Sept. 17; Arnolfini, Bristol, England, Sept. 24-Oct. 23; Midland Group, Nottingham, England, Jan. 7-Feb. 4, 1984; Museum of Modern Art, Oxford, England, Apr. 1-May 27, 1984.

Kolbowski, Silvia. "Covering Mapplethorpe's 'Lady'." *Art in America* (New York), vol. 71, no. 6, Summer, pp. 10-11.

Simson, Emily. "Portraits of a Lady." *Art News* (New York), vol. 82, no. 9, Nov., pp. 53-54.

Zelevansky, Lynn. "Robert Mapplethorpe: Leo Castelli." *Flash Art* (Milan, Italy), no. 113, Summer, pp. 63-64.

1984
Manegold, C.S. "Robert Mapplethorpe, 1970-1983; on the 1983-1984 Retrospective." *Arts Magazine* (New York), vol. 58, no. 6, Feb., pp. 96-99.

Naef, Weston and Rathbone, Belinda, ed. *The Gallery of World Photography/New Directions*, Tokyo, Japan: Shueisha Publishing Co., Ltd., pp. 36-37.

Palazzo Fortuny, Venice, Italy. *Robert Mapplethorpe fotografie*. Catalogue (Milan, Italy: Idea Books), text by Germano Celant. Traveled.

Richard Prince
photograph by Robert Mapplethorpe, March 1983

Richard Prince

The people in the entertainment pictures:

The first time I saw them, I saw them in a photograph, what they call a file or publicity pic. I had seen them before, at their job, but there, they didn't come across or measure up anywhere near as well as they did in their picture. Next to me, (in person) they were too real to look at, and what they did in daily life could never guarantee the effect of what usually came to be received from an objective resemblance. I needed them on paper, a material with a flat and seamless surface . . . a physical location which could represent their resemblance all in one place . . . a place that had the chances of looking real, but a place that didn't have any specific chances of being real.

The production of this simulation came about by ingesting, perhaps "perceiving" the fiction their photograph imagined. And what I seemed to be able to do, either in front or away from their look, was pass time in a particular bodily state, an alternating balance which turned me in and out, and made me see something that appeared to be truer than it really was . . . .

Untitled (Carole) 1982
Color photograph
30 x 44 in. (76.20 x 111.76 cm.)
Courtesy the artist

Untitled (Kristy) 1982
Color photograph
30 x 44 in. (76.20 x 111.76 cm.)
Courtesy the artist

Untitled (Laoura) 1982
Color photograph
30 x 44 in. (76.20 x 111.76 cm.)
Courtesy the artist

Untitled (Luanne) 1982
Color photograph
30 x 44 in. (76.20 x 111.76 cm.)
Courtesy the artist

Untitled (Fayy) 1983
Color photograph
30 x 44 in. (76.20 x 111.76 cm.)
Courtesy the artist

Untitled (Russell) 1983
Color photograph
30 x 44 in. (76.20 x 111.76 cm.)
Courtesy the artist

Richard Prince

One-Artist Exhibitions
1973
University Art Gallery, University of Massachusetts, Boston.

Angus Whyte Gallery, Boston, Massachusetts.

1974
Massachusetts College of Art, Boston.

Angus Whyte Gallery, Boston, Massachusetts.

1976
Ellen Sragow Gallery, New York.

Ellen Sragow Gallery, New York.

1977
Ellen Sragow Gallery, New York.

1978
Galerie Jollenbeck, Cologne, West Germany.

1979
Three Lives & Company Bookstore, New York (Window Installation).

1980
Artists Space, New York.

CEPA Gallery, Buffalo, New York.

The New Museum, New York (Window Installation).

Printed Matter, New York (Window Installation).

1981
Metro Pictures, New York.

Jancar/Kuhlenschmidt Gallery, Los Angeles, California.

1982
Metro Pictures, New York.

1983
Le Nouveau Musée, Villeurbanne, France.

Richard Kuhlenschmidt Gallery, Los Angeles, California.

Institute of Contemporary Arts, London, England.

Le Consortium, Dijon, France.

Baskerville + Watson, New York.

1984
Feature Gallery, Chicago, Illinois.

Riverside Studios, London, England.

Selected Readings
1976
Prince, Richard. "Eleven Conversations." *Tracks* (New York), vol. 2, no. 3, Fall, pp. 41-46.

1978
Lowndes, Joan. "Richard Prince: bringing the outdoors in." *Artscanada* (Toronto, Ontario, Canada), vol. 222-223, Oct.-Nov., pp. 43-47.

Prince, Richard. "From *None*." *Paris Review* (New York), no. 73, Fall, pp. 93-99.

Wooster, Ann Sargent. "Richard Prince: Ellen Sragow." *Art News* (New York), vol. 77, no. 2, Feb., p. 146.

1979
Prince, Richard. "Author's Note." *White Walls* (Chicago), no. 2, Winter-Spring.

1980
Bell, Jane. "Reviews." *Art News* (New York), vol. 79, no. 7, Sept., p. 252.

Bertolo, Diane. "Photos Make the Familiar Disturbingly Different." *Buffalo Evening News* (Buffalo), June 18, p. 38.

Kalil, Susie. "Houston Art Wave." *Artweek* (Oakland, California), Aug. 2, p. 15.

Prince, Richard. "Menthol Pictures." *Real Life Magazine* (New York), no. 4, Summer, pp. 29-31.

_____. "Moving by Wading More than Swimming." *White Walls* (Chicago), no. 4, July.

_____. "Primary Transfers." *Real Life Magazine* (New York), no. 3, Mar., pp. 2-3.

_____. *War Pictures*. New York: Artists Space.

1981
Allen Memorial Art Museum, Oberlin College, Ohio. *6 Photographers: Concept/Theater/Fiction*, Oct. 13-Nov. 22. Catalogue, text by William Olander.

Cohen, Ronny H. "Love is Blind." *Artforum* (New York), vol. 20, no. 2, Oct., p. 82.

Crimp, Douglas. "The Museum's Old/The Library's New Subject." *Parachute* (Montreal, Quebec, Canada), Spring, pp. 32-37.

_____. "The Photographic Activity of Postmodernism." *October* (Cambridge, Massachusetts), no. 15, Winter, pp. 91-101.

Drohojowska, Hunter. "Pick of the Week." *Los Angeles Weekly* (Los Angeles), Oct. 23.

Grundberg, Andy. "After A Fashion?" *The Soho Weekly News* (New York), Feb. 25-Mar. 2, p. 50.

Hayden Gallery, Massachusetts Institute of Technology, Cambridge. *Body Language: Figurative Aspects of Recent Art*, Oct. 2-Dec. 24. Catalogue, text by Roberta Smith. Traveled to The Fort Worth Art Museum, Texas, Sept. 11-Oct. 24, 1982; University of South Florida Art Gallery, Tampa, Nov. 12-Dec. 17, 1982; Contemporary Arts Center, Cincinnati, Ohio, Jan. 13-Feb. 27, 1983.

Klein, Michael. "Richard Prince." *Arts Magazine* (New York), vol. 55, no. 7, Mar., p. 9.

Knight, Christopher. "Turning the 'real' world into Art." *Los Angeles Herald Examiner* (Los Angeles), Oct. 25, p. E3.

Lawson, Thomas. "Last Exit: Painting." *Artforum* (New York), vol. 20, no. 2, Oct., pp. 40-47.

M[uchnic], S[uzanne]. "Galleries." *Los Angeles Times* (Los Angeles), Oct. 23, pp. 5-6.

Prince, Richard. "War Pictures." *ZG Magazine* (London, England), no. 3.

Rheinisches Landesmuseum, Bonn, West Germany. *Lichtbildnisse: The Portrait in Photography*, Mar. 1-June 1. Catalogue, text by Klaus Honnef.

Tatransky, Valentin. "Richard Prince/Michael Zwack." *Arts Magazine* (New York), vol. 55, no. 9, May, p. 34.

1982

Contemporary Arts Center, Cincinnati, Ohio. *Face It: 10 Contemporary Artists*, July 8-Aug. 28. Catalogue, texts by William Olander and Joanna Frueh. Organized by the Ohio Foundation on the Arts. Traveled to The Museums at Hartwick College, Oneonta, New York, Sept. 12-Oct. 16; The College of Wooster Art Museum, Ohio, Oct. 24-Nov. 21; Contemporary Art Center at Cleveland, Ohio, Dec. 3-Jan. 3, 1983; Trisolini Gallery, Ohio University, Athens, Jan. 10-Feb. 12, 1983; University of Colorado Art Galleries, Boulder, Mar. 5-Apr. 9, 1983; Freedman Galleries, Albright College, Reading, Pennsylvania, Mar. 17-June 19, 1983; Doane Hall Art Gallery, Allegheny College, Meadville, Pennsylvania, Oct. 20-Nov. 18, 1983; Southern Ohio Museum and Cultural Center, Portsmouth, Dec. 18, 1983-Jan. 28, 1984.

Deitcher, David. "Richard Prince at Metro Pictures." *Art in America* (New York), vol. 69, no. 7, Summer, p. 144.

Grundberg, Andy. "Photography View: Exploiting the Glut of Existing Imagery." *The New York Times* (New York), Jan. 31, p. D29.

Institute of Contemporary Art, University of Pennsylvania, Philadelphia. *Image Scavengers: Photography*, Dec. 8-Jan. 30, 1983. Catalogue, texts by Paula Marincola and Douglas Crimp.

Klein, Michael. "Richard Prince: Metro Pictures." *Art News* (New York), vol. 82, no. 7, Sept., pp. 155-56.

Kruger, Barbara and Prince, Richard. "All Tomorrow's Parties (A Double Conversation)." *Bomb* (New York), no. 3, pp. 42-43.

Linker, Kate. "Melodramatic Tactics." *Artforum* (New York), vol. 20, no. 1, Sept., pp. 30-32.

_____. "On Richard Prince's Photographs." *Arts Magazine* (New York), vol. 57, no. 3, Nov., pp. 120-22.

Milwaukee Art Museum, Wisconsin. *New Figuration in America*, Dec. 3-Jan. 23, 1983. Catalogue, texts by Russell Bowman and Peter Schjeldahl.

The Renaissance Society at the University of Chicago, Illinois. *A Fatal Attraction: Art and the Media*, May 12-June 12. Catalogue, text by Thomas Lawson.

Whitney Museum of American Art, Downtown Branch, New York. *Frames of Reference*, May 6-June 4. Catalogue, text by Nora Halpern.

1983

Drohojowska, Hunter. "The Genuine Simulations of Richard Prince." *Los Angeles Weekly* (Los Angeles), Apr. 15-21, p. 24.

_____. "Richard Prince." *Flash Art* (Milan, Italy), no. 113, Summer, p. 66.

_____. "The Ultimate Ironic Time." *Los Angeles Weekly* (Los Angeles), Dec. 30, pp. 26-27.

Glueck, Grace. "Artists Who 'Scavenge' from the Media." *The New York Times* (New York), Jan. 9, pp. H29-30.

Grundberg, Andy. "Photography View." *The New York Times* (New York), May 8, pp. H31, H36.

Kuspit, Donald B. "New Figuration in America at the Milwaukee Art Museum." *Art in America* (New York), vol. 71, no. 8, Sept., pp. 178-79.

Liebmann, Lisa. "Science Fiction, John Weber Gallery." *Artforum* (New York), vol. 22, no. 4, Dec., pp. 74-75.

Linker, Kate. "Borrowed Time, Baskerville + Watson." *Artforum* (New York), vol. 21, no. 9, May, p. 100.

_____. "On Artificiality." *Flash Art* (Milan, Italy), no. 111, Mar., pp. 33-35.

Newman, Michael. "Richard Prince and the Uncanny." *Art Monthly* (London, England), no. 72, Dec.-Jan. 1984.

Le Nouveau Musée, Villeurbanne, France. *Pamphlet: Richard Prince*, Jan. 21-Mar. 3. Catalogue, text by Kate Linker.

Prince, Richard. "Why I Go to the Movies Alone." *Journal* (Los Angeles), no. 37, vol. 4, Sept-Oct., pp. 41-49.

Smith, Roberta. "Appropriation über Alles." *The Village Voice* (New York), Jan. 11, p. 73.

1984

Artists Space, New York. *A Decade of New Art*, May 31-June 30. Catalogue, text by Linda L. Cathcart.

Bernard, April and Thompson, Mimi. "Video Tunes In." *Vanity Fair* (New York), vol. 47, no. 2, Feb., pp. 30-31.

Fisher, Jean. "Richard Prince, Baskerville + Watson." *Artforum* (New York), vol. 22, no. 5, Jan., p. 75.

Grundberg, Andy. "The New Modern Reenters the Contemporary Arena." *The New York Times* (New York), May 27, pp. 27, 32.

Halley, Peter. "Richard Prince Interviewed." *ZG Magazine* (New York), no. 10, Spring.

Howe, Katherine. "Science Fiction at John Weber." *Images & Issues* (Santa Monica, California), vol. 4, no. 4, Jan.-Feb.

Schaves, Frances. "Richard Prince's Photographs." *Express* (New York), Winter, p. 7.

Smith, Roberta and Levin, Kim. "We Remember MOMA." *The Village Voice* (New York), May 22, pp. 89, 92.

David Salle
photograph by Robert Mapplethorpe, March 1983

David Salle

These images are as literal as they are not. You don't have to be reading the newspaper on the train, but you're on the train with a newspaper.

Zeitgeist Painting #2 1982
Oil and acrylic on canvas
156 x 117 in. (396.24 x 297.18 cm.)
Collection Jerry and Emily Spiegel

Concave Warrior 1983
Oil and acrylic on canvas and chair legs
117 x 108 in. (297.18 x 274.32 cm.)
Collection the artist
Courtesy Mary Boone Gallery, New York

93

King Kong 1983
Acrylic and oil on canvas, platform and bulb
123 x 96 x 26 in. (312.42 x 243.84 x 66.04 cm.)
Collection Mr. and Mrs. Bagley Wright

David Salle

One-Artist Exhibitions
1975
Project, Inc., Cambridge, Massachusetts.

Claire S. Copley Gallery, Los Angeles, California.

1976
Fondation Corps de Garde, Groningen, The Netherlands.

Artists Space, New York.

1977
Fondation de Appel, Amsterdam, The Netherlands.

The Kitchen, New York.

1978
Fondation Corps de Garde, Groningen, The Netherlands.

1979
Anna Leonowens Gallery, Nova Scotia College of Art and Design, Halifax, Canada.

Gagosian/Nosei-Weber Gallery, New York.

The Kitchen, New York.

1980
Fondation de Appel, Amsterdam, The Netherlands.

Annina Nosei Gallery, New York.

Galerie Bruno Bischofberger, Zurich, Switzerland.

1981
Mary Boone Gallery, New York.

Larry Gagosian Gallery, Los Angeles, California.

Lucio Amelio Gallery, Naples, Italy.

1982
Mario Diacono Gallery, Rome, Italy.

Mary Boone Gallery and Leo Castelli Gallery, New York.

Galerie Bruno Bischofberger, Zurich, Switzerland.

Anthony d'Offay Gallery, London, England.

American Graffiti Gallery, Amsterdam, The Netherlands.

1983
Akira Ikeda Gallery, Tokyo, Japan.

Ronald Greenberg Gallery, St. Louis, Missouri.

Museum Boymans-van Beuningen, Rotterdam, The Netherlands.

Mary Boone Gallery, New York.

Castelli Graphics, New York.

Galerie Ascan Crone, Hamburg, West Germany.

Galerie Schellman & Kluser, Munich, West Germany.

Addison Gallery of American Art, Andover, Massachusetts.

Larry Gagosian Gallery, Los Angeles, California.

1984
Leo Castelli Gallery, New York.

Galerie Bruno Bischofberger, Zurich, Switzerland.

Mario Diacono Gallery, Rome, Italy.

Selected Readings
1974
Baker, Kenneth. "It's the Thought That Counts." *The Boston Phoenix* (Boston), Sept. 24.

Burgin, Richard. "The Impact of Conceptual Art at Project, Inc." *The Boston Globe* (Boston), Sept. 17.

1975
Askey, Ruth. "On Video: Banality, Sex, Cooking." *Artweek* (Oakland, California), Aug. 9, p.5.

1976
Robbe, Lon de Vries. "David Salle." *Museumjournal* (Amsterdam, The Netherlands), vol. 21, Sept., pp. 107-10.

1979
Lawson, Thomas. "The Uses of Representation: Making Some Distinctions." *Flash Art* (Milan, Italy), no. 88-89, Mar.-Apr., pp.37-39.

Rickey, Carrie. "Voice Choices: David Salle." *The Village Voice* (New York), Nov. 21, p. 63.

Tatransky, Valentin. "Intelligence and the Desire to Draw: On David Salle." *Real Life Magazine* (New York), vol. 2, Nov., pp. 6-7.

Zimmer, William. "Who Puts Women on a Pedestal?" *The Soho Weekly News* (New York), Nov. 15.

1980
Brooke Alexander Inc., New York. *Illustration & Allegory*, May 13-June 14. Catalogue, text by Carter Ratcliff.

Hess, Elizabeth. "Barefoot Girls with Cheek Gloss." *The Village Voice* (New York), Nov. 19, p. 93.

Kertess, Klaus. "Figuring It Out." *Artforum* (New York), vol. 19, no. 3, Nov., pp. 31-35.

Lawson, Thomas. "David Salle." *Flash Art* (Milan, Italy), no. 94-95, Jan.-Feb., p. 33.

1980 (continued)

Rickey, Carrie. "Advance to the Rear Guard." *The Village Voice* (New York), Aug. 27, p. 66.

_____. "Naive Nouveau and its Malcontents." *Flash Art* (Milan, Italy), no. 98-99, Summer, pp. 36-39.

Robinson, Walter. "David Salle at Gagosian/Nosei-Weber." *Art in America* (New York), vol. 68, no. 3, Mar., pp. 117-18.

Salle, David. "Images that Understand Us: A Conversation with David Salle and James Welling." *Journal* (Los Angeles), no. 27, vol. 3, June-July, pp. 41-44.

Simon, Joan. "Double Takes." *Art in America* (New York), vol. 68, no. 8, Oct., pp. 113-17.

Tatransky, Valentin. "David Salle." *Arts Magazine* (New York), vol. 54, no. 6, Feb., p. 37.

1981

Albright-Knox Art Gallery, CEPA Gallery and HALLWALLS, Buffalo, New York. *Figures: Forms and Expressions,* Nov. 20-Jan. 3, 1982. Catalogue, text by G. Roger Denson, Biff Henrich, Charlotta Kotik and Susan Krane.

Allen Memorial Art Museum, Oberlin College, Ohio. *Young Americans,* Apr. 1-May 3. Catalogue, texts by Douglas Crimp, Joanna Frueh, William Olander and Carter Ratcliff.

Drohojowska, Hunter. "Pick of the Week." *Los Angeles Weekly* (Los Angeles), Apr. 24.

Hammond, Pamela. "David Salle at Larry Gagosian." *Images and Issues* (Santa Monica, California), vol. 2, no. 2, Fall, pp. 60-61.

Hayden Gallery, Massachusetts Institute of Technology, Cambridge. *Body Language: Figurative Aspects of Recent Art,* Oct. 2-Dec. 24. Catalogue, text by Roberta Smith. Traveled to The Fort Worth Art Museum, Texas, Sept. 11-Oct. 24, 1982; University of South Florida Art Gallery, Tampa, Nov. 12-Dec. 17, 1982; Contemporary Arts Center, Cincinnati, Ohio, Jan. 13-Feb. 27, 1983.

Hubert, Christian; Levine, Sherrie; Owens, Craig; Salle, David; Schnabel, Julian. "Post Modernism: A Symposium." *Real Life Magazine* (New York), no. 6, Summer, pp. 4-10.

Knight, Christopher. "The Medium Cool Art of David Salle." *Los Angeles Herald Examiner* (Los Angeles), May 3, p. E6.

Lawson, Thomas. "David Salle at Mary Boone." *Artforum* (New York), vol. 19, no. 9, May, pp. 71-72.

_____. "Last Exit: Painting." *Artforum* (New York), vol. 20, no. 2, Oct., pp. 40-47.

Levine, Sherrie. "David Salle." *Flash Art* (Milan, Italy), no. 103, Summer, p. 34.

Marzorati, Gerald. "Art Picks: Salle/Schnabel." *The Soho Weekly News* (New York), June 24-30, p. 36.

Pincus-Witten, Robert. "Entries: Sheer Grunge." *Arts Magazine* (New York), vol. 55, no. 9, May, pp. 93-97.

Ratcliff, Carter. "Westkunst: David Salle." *Flash Art* (Milan, Italy), no. 103, Summer, pp. 33-34.

Ricard, René. "Not About Julian Schnabel." *Artforum* (New York), vol. 19, no. 10, Summer, pp. 74-80.

Schjeldahl, Peter. "David Salle Interview." *Journal* (Los Angeles), no. 30, vol. 3, Sept.-Oct., pp. 15-21.

Siegel, Jeanne. "David Salle: Interpretation of Image." *Arts Magazine* (New York), vol. 55, no. 8, Apr., pp. 94-95.

Smith, Roberta. "Separation Anxieties." *The Village Voice* (New York), Mar. 18, p. 78.

Wilson, William. "David Salle." *Los Angeles Times* (Los Angeles), Apr. 24, part 6, p. 9.

Yoskowitz, Robert. "David Salle." *Arts Magazine* (New York), vol. 56, no. 1, Sept., p. 31.

1982

Goldberg, RoseLee. "Post-TV Art." *Portfolio* (New York), vol. 4, no. 4, July-Aug., pp. 76-79.

Groot, Paul. "David Salle." *Flash Art* (Milan, Italy), no. 109, Nov., pp. 68, 70.

Institute of Contemporary Art, University of Pennsylvania, Philadelphia. *Image Scavengers: Painting,* Dec. 8-Jan. 30, 1983. Catalogue, text by Janet Kardon.

Kassel, West Germany. *Documenta 7.* Catalogue.

Kontova, Helena. "From Performance to Painting." *Flash Art* (Milan, Italy), no. 106, Feb.-Mar., pp. 16-21.

Kuspit, Donald. "David Salle at Mary Boone and Castelli." *Art in America* (New York), vol. 70, no. 7, Summer, p. 142.

Larson, Kay. "David Salle." *New York Magazine* (New York), Mar. 29, p. 77.

Liebmann, Lisa. "David Salle." *Artforum* (New York), vol. 20, no. 11, Summer, pp. 89-90.

Martin-Gropius-Bau, West Berlin, Germany. *Zeitgeist.* Catalogue, texts by Christos M. Joachimedes, Robert Rosenblum, Hilton Kramer, Walter Bachauer, Karl-Heinz Bohrer, Paul Feyerabend, Vittorio Magnago Lampugnani and Thomas Bernhard.

Owens, Craig. "Back to the Studio." *Art in America* (New York), vol. 70, no. 1, Jan., p. 34.

Pincus-Witten, Robert. "David Salle: Holiday Glassware." *Arts Magazine* (New York), vol. 56, no. 8, Apr., pp. 58-60.

Ratcliff, Carter. "Contemporary American Art." *Flash Art* (Milan, Italy), no. 108, Summer, pp. 32-35.

_____. "David Salle." *Interview* (New York), vol. 12, no. 2, Feb., pp. 64-66.

The Renaissance Society at the University of Chicago, Illinois. *A Fatal Attraction: Art and the Media,* May 2 - June 12. Catalogue, text by Thomas Lawson.

Russell, John. "Art: David Salle." *The New York Times* (New York), Mar. 19, p. C24.

Schjeldahl, Peter. "David Salle's Objects of Disaffection." *The Village Voice* (New York), Mar. 23, p. 83.

Walker Art Center, Minneapolis, Minnesota. *Eight Artists: The Anxious Edge,* Apr. 25-June 13. Catalogue, text by Lisa Lyons.

Yoskowitz, Robert. "David Salle at Mary Boone." *Arts Magazine* (New York), vol. 57, no. 1, Sept., p. 34.

1983

Akira Ikeda Gallery, Tokyo, Japan. *David Salle*, Jan. 17-Feb. 28. Catalogue, text by Maki Kuwayama.

Ashbery, John. "Biennials Bloom in the Spring." *Newsweek* (New York), Apr. 18, pp. 93-94.

Blau, Douglas. "Kim MacConnel; David Salle." *Arts Magazine* (New York), vol. 57, no. 5, Jan., pp. 62-63.

Dimitrijevic, Nena. "David Salle, Anthony d'Offay." *Flash Art* (Milan, Italy), no. 111, Mar., p. 66.

Galerie Ascan Crone, Hamburg, West Germany. *David Salle: New Paintings and Watercolors*, Sept. 22-Oct. 22. Catalogue, text by Michael Kruger.

Galerie Schellman & Kluser, Munich, West Germany. *David Salle, Francis Picabia*, Sept. 29-Oct. 30. Catalogue, text by Ingrid Rein.

Glueck, Grace. "Art: Big American Figure Drawings." *The New York Times* (New York), Mar. 18, p. C23.

_____. "Artists Who 'Scavenge' from the Media." *The New York Times* (New York), Jan. 9, pp. H29-30.

Hirshhorn Museum and Sculpture Garden, Washington, D.C. *Directions 1983*, Mar. 10-May 15. Catalogue, text by Phyllis D. Rosenzweig.

Hughes, Robert. "Three From the Image Machine." *Time Magazine* (New York), Mar. 14, pp. 83-84.

Levin, Kim. "Double Takes." *The Village Voice* (New York), Apr. 26, pp. 91-108.

Liebmann, Lisa. "David Salle, Mary Boone Gallery." *Artforum* (New York), vol. 21, no. 10, June, p. 74.

Morgan, Stuart. "David Salle at Anthony d'Offay." *Artscribe* (London, England), no. 39, Feb., pp. 51-53.

Moufarrege, Nicolas. "David Salle." *Flash Art* (Milan, Italy), no. 112, May, p. 60.

Museum Boymans-van Beuningen, Rotterdam, The Netherlands. *David Salle*, Feb. 26-Apr. 17. Catalogue, texts by W.A.L. Beeren and Carter Ratcliff.

Nilson, Lisbet. "Making It Neo." *Art News* (New York), vol. 82, no. 7, Sept., pp. 62-70.

Raynor, Vivien. "David Salle." *The New York Times* (New York), Feb. 18, p. C24.

Roberts, John. "An Interview with David Salle." *Art Monthly* (London, England), Mar., pp. 3-7.

Schjeldahl, Peter. "Falling in Style, The New Art and Our Discontents." *Vanity Fair* (New York), vol. 46, no. 1, Mar., pp. 115-17.

Smith, Roberta. "Appropriation über Alles." *The Village Voice* (New York), Jan. 11, p. 73.

_____. "Comics Stripped." *The Village Voice* (New York), Aug. 23, pp. 94-100.

_____. "Making Impressions." *The Village Voice* (New York), Mar. 1, p. 79.

Starenko, Michael. "What's an Artist to Do? A Short History of Postmodernism and Photography." *Afterimage* (New York), vol. 10, no. 6, Jan., pp. 4-5.

Whitney Museum of American Art, New York. *1983 Biennial Exhibition*, Mar. 15-May 22. Catalogue.

1984

Artists Space, New York. *A Decade of New Art*, May 31-June 30. Catalogue, text by Linda L. Cathcart.

"Francis Picabia and David Salle." *Flash Art* (Milan, Italy), no. 115, Jan., p. 31.

Hicks, Emily. "The Provocative Work of David Salle." *Artweek* (Oakland, California), Jan. 14, p. 1.

La Jolla Museum of Contemporary Art, California. *American Art Since 1970*, Mar. 10-Apr. 22. Catalogue, text by Richard Marshall. Organized by the Whitney Museum of American Art, New York. Traveled to Museo Tamayo, Mexico City, Mexico, May 17-July 29; North Carolina Museum of Art, Raleigh, Sept. 29-Nov. 25; Sheldon Memorial Art Gallery, University of Nebraska, Lincoln, Jan. 12-Mar. 3, 1985; Center for the Fine Arts, Miami, Florida, Mar. 30-May 26, 1985.

Marzorati, Gerald. "The Artful Dodger." *Arts Magazine* (New York), vol. 83, no. 6, Summer, pp. 47-55.

The Museum of Modern Art, New York. *An International Survey of Recent Painting and Sculpture*, May 17-Aug. 19. Catalogue.

Pincus-Witten, Robert. "Entries: I-Know-That-You-Know-That-I-Know." *Arts Magazine* (New York), vol. 58, no. 6, Feb., pp. 126-29.

San Francisco Museum of Modern Art, California. *The Human Condition: SFMMA Biennial III*, June 28-Aug. 26. Catalogue, texts by Dorothy Martinson, Wolfgang Max Faust, Achille Bonita Oliva, Klaus Ottmann, Edward Kienholz.

Schwartz, Manford. "David Salle." *The New Yorker* (New York), Apr. 30, pp. 104-11.

Smith, Roberta. "Quality Is the Best Revenge." *The Village Voice* (New York), Apr. 3, p. 79.

Julian Schnabel
photograph by Robert Mapplethorpe, March 1983

Julian Schnabel

Starved with pain, solomonic, proper,
he was howling; circumspect, over-suspicious, perjured,
he was going, he was coming back, he was answering; he was daring,
fatidic, scarlet, irresistible.

In society, in glass, in dust, in coal,
he took off; he wavered, in speaking in gold; he went up in flames,
he rolled over, in respect;
in velvet, in weeping, he fell back.

To remember? To insist? To leave? To pardon?
Scowling he would come to
rest, rough, aghast, mural;
he was meditating to engrave himself, to become confused, to perish.

Unattackably, with impunity,
blackly, he will sniff, he will understand;
he will orally dress;
uncertainly he will go, he will turn coward, he will forget.

26 September 1937

Transido, salomónico, decente,
ululaba; compuesto, caviloso, cadavérico, perjuro,
iba, tornaba, respondía; osaba,
fatídico, escarlata, irresistible.

En sociedad, en vidrio, en polvo, en hulla,
marchóse; vaciló, en hablando en oro; fulguró,
volteó, en acatamiento;
en terciopelo, en llanto, replegóse.

¿Recordar? ¿Insistir? ¿Ir? ¿Perdonar?
Ceñudo, acabaría
recostado, áspero, atónito, mural;
meditaba estamparse, confundirse, fenecer.

Inatacablemente, impunemente,
negramente, husmeará, comprenderá;
vestiráse oralmente;
inciertamente irá, acobardaráse, olvidará.

26 septiembre 1937

From Cesar Vallejo, *Poemas Humanos*, translated by Clayton Eshleman (New York: Grove Press, Inc., 1968), pp. 188-89.

Procession (for Jean Vigo) 1979
Oil on wood
110 x 86 in. (279.40 x 218.44 cm.)
Private collection, New York

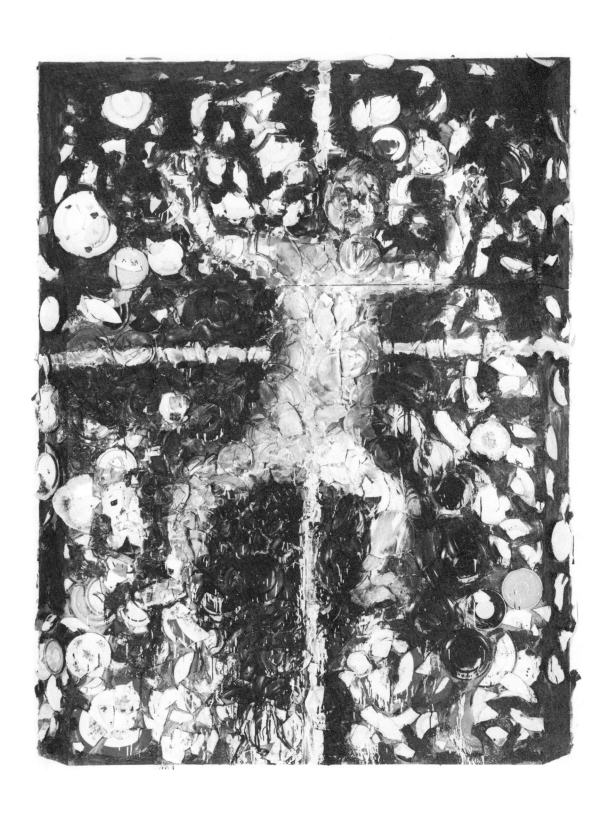

Portrait of My Daughter 1982
Plates, bondo and oil on wood
108 x 84 in. (274.32 x 213.36 cm.)
Private collection, New York

101

Maria Callas 3 1983
Oil on velvet
108 x 120 in. (274.32 x 304.80 cm.)
Private collection, New York

Julian Schnabel

One-Artist Exhibitions
1976
Contemporary Arts Museum, Houston, Texas.

1978
Galerie December, Dusseldorf, West Germany.

1979
Mary Boone Gallery, New York.

Daniel Weinberg Gallery, San Francisco, California.

Mary Boone Gallery, New York.

1980
Galerie Bruno Bischofberger, Zurich, Switzerland.

Young/Hoffman Gallery, Chicago, Illinois.

1981
Mary Boone Gallery and Leo Castelli Gallery, New York.

Anthony d'Offay Gallery, London, England.

Kunsthalle, Basel, Switzerland. Circulated.

1982
Stedelijk Museum, Amsterdam, The Netherlands.

Galerie Bruno Bischofberger, Zurich, Switzerland.

Margo Leavin Gallery, Los Angeles, California.

Los Angeles County Museum of Art, Los Angeles, California.

Daniel Weinberg Gallery, San Francisco, California.

University Art Museum, Berkeley, California.

Tate Gallery, London, England.

Mary Boone Gallery, New York.

1983
Leo Castelli Gallery, New York.

Galerie Daniel Templon, Paris, France.

1984
Akira Ikeda Gallery, Tokyo, Japan.

Galerie Bruno Bischofberger, Zurich, Switzerland.

Selected Readings
1975
DeAk, Edit. "Julian Schnabel." *ART-RITE Magazine* (New York), May, p. 19.

1976
Moser, Charlotte. "Houston: Between Fantasy and Surrealism." *Art News* (New York), vol. 75, no. 4, Apr., p. 66.

1979
Anderson, Ali. "Voice Choices: Julian Schnabel." *The Village Voice* (New York), Feb. 26, p. 55.

Reed, Dupuy Warrick. "Julian Schnabel: The Truth of the Moment." *Arts Magazine* (New York), vol. 54, no. 3, Nov., p. 86.

Ricard, René. "Julian Schnabel's Plate Painting at Mary Boone." *Art in America* (New York), vol. 67, no. 10, Nov., p. 125.

Rickey, Carrie. "Julian Schnabel." *Artforum* (New York), vol. 17, no. 9, May, p. 59.

_____. "Voice Choices: Julian Schnabel." *The Village Voice* (New York), Nov. 21, p. 63.

Tatransky, Valentin. "Julian Schnabel." *Artforum* (New York), vol. 17, no. 9, May, p. 36.

Zimmer, William. "Julian Schnabel: New Painting." *The Soho Weekly News* (New York), Feb. 22-28, p. 31.

_____. "Plats du Jour." *The Soho Weekly News* (New York), Nov. 22-28, p. 20.

1980

Kertess, Klaus. "Figuring it Out." *Artforum* (New York), vol. 19, no. 3, Nov., pp. 30-35.

Ratcliff, Carter. "Art to Art: Julian Schnabel." *Interview* (New York), vol. 10, no. 10, Oct., pp. 55-57.

Shore, Michael. "How Does it Look? How Does it Sound?" *Art News* (New York), vol. 79, no. 9, Nov., pp. 78-85.

Yoskowitz, Robert. "Julian Schnabel." *Arts Magazine* (New York), vol. 54, no. 6, Feb., p. 28.

Zimmer, William. "Artbreakers: New York's Emerging Artists." *The Soho Weekly News* (New York), Sept. 17-23, pp. 35-45.

1981

Atkins, Robert. "Julian Schnabel at Mary Boone and Castelli." *Images and Issues* (Santa Monica, California), vol. 2, no. 2, Fall, pp. 56-57.

Cavaliere, Barbara. "Julian Schnabel." *Arts Magazine* (New York), vol. 55, no. 10, June, pp. 34-35.

Hayden Gallery, Massachusetts Institute of Technology, Cambridge. *Body Language: Figurative Aspects of Recent Art,* Oct. 2-Dec. 24. Catalogue, text by Roberta Smith. Traveled to The Fort Worth Art Museum, Texas, Sept. 11-Oct. 24, 1982; University of South Florida Art Gallery, Tampa, Nov. 12-Dec. 17, 1982; Contemporary Arts Center, Cincinnati, Ohio, Jan. 13-Feb. 27, 1983.

Hubert, Christian; Levine, Sherrie; Owens, Craig; Salle, David; Schnabel, Julian. "Post Modernism: A Symposium." *Real Life Magazine* (New York), no. 6, Sept., pp. 4-10.

Kramer, Hilton. "An Audacious Inaugural Exhibition." *The New York Times* (New York), Sept. 20, pp. D33-34.

_____. "Art: Two Painters Explore New Wave." *The New York Times* (New York), Apr. 17, p. C18.

Kunsthalle, Basel, Switzerland. *Julian Schnabel,* Oct. 3-Nov. 15. Catalogue, text by Jean-Christophe Ammann and Carter Ratcliff. Traveled to Frankfurter Kunstverein, Frankfurt, West Germany, Dec. 18-Jan. 31, 1982; Louisiana Museum, Humlebaek, Denmark, Mar. 13-May 2, 1982.

Levin, Kim. "Art: Julian Schnabel." *The Village Voice* (New York), Apr. 15-21, p. 64.

Marzorati, Gerald. "Art Picks: Julian Schnabel." *The Soho Weekly News* (New York), Apr. 15-21.

Perrault, John. "Is Julian Schnabel that Good?" *The Soho Weekly News* (New York), Apr. 22-28, p. 63.

Phillips, Deborah C. "Julian Schnabel." *Art News* (New York), vol. 80, no. 8, Oct., p. 218.

Ricard, René. "Not About Julian Schnabel." *Artforum* (New York), vol. 19, no. 10, Summer, pp. 74-80, cover.

Royal Academy of Arts, London, England. *A New Spirit in Painting,* Jan. 15-Mar. 18. Catalogue, texts by Christos M. Joachimedes, Norman Rosenthal and Nicholas Serota.

S[tephens], M[ark]. "Bull in the China Shop." *Newsweek* (New York), May 11, p. 79.

Sundell, Nina. "Westkunst: Julian Schnabel." *Flash Art* (Milan, Italy), no. 103, Summer, p. 32.

Whitney Museum of American Art, New York. *1981 Biennial Exhibition,* Jan. 20-Apr. 19. Catalogue.

Yoskowitz, Robert. "Julian Schnabel." *Arts Magazine* (New York), vol. 56, no. 1, Sept., p. 29.

1982

Atkins, Robert. "Julian Schnabel: The Agony and the Ecstasy." *The San Francisco Bay Guardian* (San Francisco), June 2.

Boettger, Suzaan. "East Coast Star's Dynamic Novelty." *The San Francisco Chronicle* (San Francisco), June 25.

Geelhaar, Christian. "Julian Schnabel's Head (For Albert)." *Arts Magazine* (New York), vol. 57, no. 2, Oct., pp. 74-75.

Glueck, Grace. "Art: Julian Schnabel Breaks Rules and Plates." *The New York Times* (New York), Oct. 8, p. C22.

The Holy Ghost Writers. "Condensation and Dish-Placement." *Real Life Magazine* (New York), no. 9, Winter 1982/83, pp. 9-13.

Hughes, Robert. "Expressionist Bric-a-Brac." *Time Magazine* (New York), Nov. 1, p. 71.

Knight, Christopher. "Descending Into the Maelstrom of a Schnabel Plate Painting." *Los Angeles Herald Examiner* (Los Angeles), Apr. 18, p. E4.

Martin-Gropius-Bau, West Berlin, Germany. *Zeitgeist.* Catalogue, texts by Christos M. Joachimedes, Robert Rosenblum, Hilton Kramer, Walter Bachauer, Karl-Heinz Bohrer, Paul Feyerabend, Vittorio Magnago Lampugnani and Thomas Bernhard.

McGuigan, Cathleen. "Julian Schnabel." *Art News* (New York), vol. 81, no. 6, Summer, pp. 88-94.

Pincus-Witten, Robert. "Julian Schnabel: Blind Faith." *Arts Magazine* (New York), vol. 55, no. 6, Feb., pp. 152-55.

The Renaissance Society at the University of Chicago, Illinois. *A Fatal Attraction: Art and the Media,* May 2-June 12. Catalogue, text by Thomas Lawson.

Roder, Sylvie. "Julian Schnabel: amplifying the risks." *Artweek* (Oakland, California), June 19, pp. 1, 20.

Schjeldahl, Peter. "The Ardor of Ambition." *The Village Voice* (New York), Feb. 23, p. 79.

Singerman, Howard. "Toward an Essay Entitled 'Restoration Comedies'." *Journal* (Los Angeles), no. 33, vol. 4, Summer, pp. 48-51.

Smith, Roberta. "Schnabel the Vincible." *The Village Voice* (New York), Nov. 2, p. 81.

Stedelijk Museum, Amsterdam, The Netherlands. *Julian Schnabel*, Jan. 28-Mar. 14. Catalogue, texts by René Ricard and Alexander van Gravenstein.

Wilson, William. "Schnabel Makes His Local Debut." *The Los Angeles Times* (Los Angeles), Apr. 9, part IV, pp. 1-2.

1983

Gambrell, Jamey. "Julian Schnabel at Castelli Greene St." *Art in America* (New York), vol. 71, no. 9, Oct., pp. 179-80.

Hapgood, Susan. "Julian Schnabel: Leo Castelli." *Flash Art* (Milan, Italy), no. 113, Summer, pp. 62-63.

Hirshhorn Museum and Sculpture Garden, Washington, D.C. *Directions 1983*, Mar. 10-May 15. Catalogue, text by Phyllis D. Rosenzweig.

Liebmann, Lisa. "Julian Schnabel, Mary Boone Gallery." *Artforum* (New York), vol. 21, no. 5, Jan., pp. 72-73.

Mohr, Dorian. "Julian Schnabel: Another Look." *Studio International* (London, England), vol. 196, no. 1000, July, pp. 8-9.

Nilson, Lisbet. "Making It Neo." *Art News* (New York), vol. 82, no. 7, Sept., pp. 62-70.

Siegel, Jeanne. "Julian Schnabel." *Arts Magazine* (New York), vol. 57, no. 10, June, p. 15.

Silverthorne, Jeanne. "Julian Schnabel." *Artforum* (New York), vol. 22, no. 1, Sept. pp. 74-75.

Whitney Museum of American Art, New York. *1983 Biennial Exhibition*, Mar. 15-May 22. Catalogue.

1984

La Jolla Museum of Contemporary Art, California. *American Art Since 1970*, Mar. 10-Apr. 22. Catalogue, text by Richard Marshall. Organized by the Whitney Museum of American Art, New York. Traveled to Museo Tamayo, Mexico City, Mexico, May 17-July 29; North Carolina Museum of Art, Raleigh, Sept. 29-Nov. 25; Sheldon Memorial Art Gallery, University of Nebraska, Lincoln, Jan. 12-Mar. 3, 1985; Center for the Fine Arts, Miami, Florida, Mar. 30-May 26, 1985.

The Museum of Modern Art, New York. *An International Survey of Recent Painting and Sculpture*, May 17-Aug. 19. Catalogue.

Schnabel, Julian. "The Patient and His Doctors." *Artforum* (New York), vol. 22, no. 6, Feb., pp. 54-59.

Zacharopoulos, Denys. "Julian Schnabel, Galerie Daniel Templon." *Artforum* (New York), vol. 22, no. 8, Apr., pp. 90-91.

Cindy Sherman
photograph by Robert Mapplethorpe, March 1983

Cindy Sherman

These were not meant to be finished portraits but were originally studies of light and how it can affect a mood. My influences and the resulting works are moving closer to real life than fictitious film stills or portraits. More inner acting is demanded to imply an exterior situation outside the zoomed-in non-action of character. Androgynous and more varied characterizations are one goal. Since this work I've been adding more humorous and uglier types.

Now trying to overcome the natural desire to hide truly hideous examples, I learn to completely objectify the possibilities of what one's body can do or look like.

I bore very quickly of work I've finished. As I write this it is two years since I finished these photos; by the time this is published it will be well over that. By then I will have completed more than a new body of work.

I don't know what I'll be doing in the future. I would like to be able to say that I'm not going to use myself anymore, not use figures, not make photos. I'd like to be doing something totally different. But I actually doubt that.

Untitled 1982
Color photograph
38 x 24 in. (96.52 x 60.96 cm.)
Courtesy the artist and Metro Pictures, New York

Untitled 1982
Color photograph
45¹/₄ x 30 in. (114.94 x 76.20 cm.)
Courtesy the artist and Metro Pictures, New York

Untitled 1982
Color photograph
45¹/₄ x 30 in. (114.94 x 76.20 cm.)
Courtesy the artist and Metro Pictures, New York

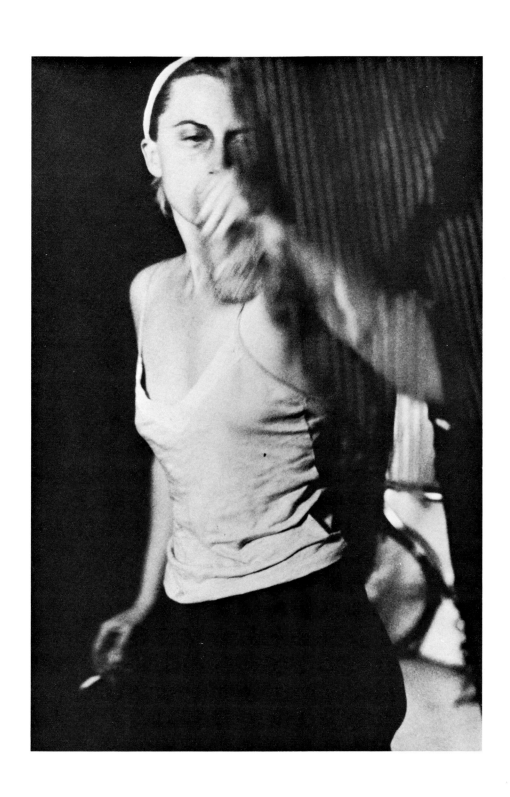

Untitled 1982
Color photograph
45¹/₄ x 30 in. (114.94 x 76.20 cm.)
Courtesy the artist and Metro Pictures, New York

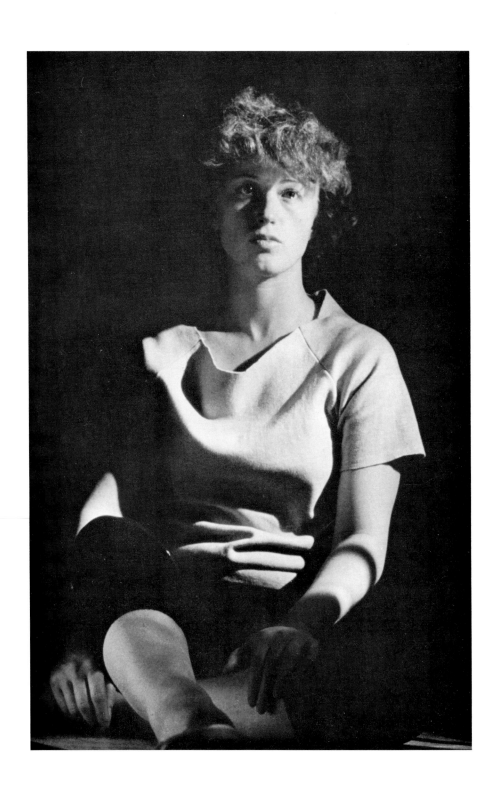

Untitled 1982
Color photograph
45¼ x 30 in. (114.94 x 76.20 cm.)
Courtesy the artist and Metro Pictures, New York

Untitled 1983
Color photograph
34³/₄ x 16¹/₂ in. (88.27 x 41.91 cm.)
Courtesy the artist and Metro Pictures, New York

Untitled 1983
Color photograph
35¼ x 21¼ in. (89.54 x 53.98 cm.)
Courtesy the artist and Metro Pictures, New York

Cindy Sherman

One-Artist Exhibitions
1976
HALLWALLS, Buffalo, New York.

1977
HALLWALLS, Buffalo, New York.

Visual Studies Workshop, Rochester, New York.

1979
HALLWALLS, Buffalo, New York.

1980
Contemporary Arts Museum, Houston, Texas.

The Kitchen, New York.

Metro Pictures, New York.

1981
Saman Gallery, Genoa, Italy.

Metro Pictures, New York.

Young/Hoffman Gallery, Chicago, Illinois.

1982
Texas Gallery, Houston.

Galerie Chantal Crousel, Paris, France.

Larry Gagosian Gallery, Los Angeles, California.

Carl Solway Gallery, Cincinnati, Ohio.

Metro Pictures, New York.

Galerie Déjà Vu, Dijon, France.

Stedelijk Museum, Amsterdam, The Netherlands. Circulated.

1983
Fay Gold Gallery, Atlanta, Georgia.

The St. Louis Art Museum, Missouri.

Galerie Schellmann & Kluser, Munich, West Germany.

Art Gallery, Fine Arts Center, State University of New York at Stony Brook. Circulated.

Metro Pictures, New York.

Rhona Hoffman Gallery, Chicago, Illinois.

Musée d'Art et d'Industrie de Saint-Etienne, France.

1984
Seibu Gallery of Contemporary Art, Tokyo, Japan.

Akron Art Museum, Ohio.

Selected Readings
1977
Albright-Knox Art Gallery, Buffalo, New York. *In Western New York*, Mar. 26-Apr. 17. Catalogue.

1979
Cathcart, Linda L. "The Western Image in New York: Longo, Sherman, Zwack." *Arts Quarterly* (New Orleans, Louisiana), no. 1, Oct.-Nov.-Dec., pp. 8-9.

"Cindy Sherman: Recent Pictures." *Sun & Moon* (College Park, Maryland), no. 8, Fall, pp. 129-36.

Crimp, Douglas. "Pictures." *October* (Cambridge, Massachusetts), no. 8, Spring, pp. 75-88.

Tatransky, Valentin. "Cindy Sherman: Artists Space." *Arts Magazine* (New York), vol. 53, no. 5, Jan., p. 19.

Upton Gallery, State University College, Buffalo, New York. *HALLWALLS: 5 Years*, Nov. 5-15. Catalogue, text by Linda L. Cathcart. Organized by The New Museum, New York. Traveled to A Space, Toronto, Ontario, Canada, Feb. 16-Mar. 8, 1980; Parsons School of Art Gallery, New York, June 20-July 18, 1980.

1980
Bishop, Joseph. "Desperate Character." *Real Life Magazine* (New York), no. 4, Summer, pp. 8-10.

Contemporary Arts Museum, Houston, Texas. *Cindy Sherman: Photographs*, Feb. 2-Mar. 23. Catalogue, text by Linda L. Cathcart.

Crossley, Mimi. "The mysterious art of Cindy Sherman at the CAM." *The Houston Post* (Houston), Feb. 10, p. 10AA.

Grundberg, Andy. "Artbreakers." *The Soho Weekly News* (New York), Sept. 17-23, p. 37.

————. "Lies for the Eyes." *The Soho Weekly News* (New York), Dec. 17-23, p. 28.

Lifson, Ben. "Masquerading." *The Village Voice* (New York), Mar. 31, p. 77.

Owens, Craig. "The Allegorical Impulse: toward a theory of postmodernism, parts I and II." *October* (Cambridge, Massachusetts), vol. 12; 13, Spring; Summer, pp. 67-86; 59-80.

Shore, Michael. "How Does It Look? How Does It Sound?" *Art News* (New York), vol. 79, no. 9, Nov., pp. 78-85.

Simon, Joan. "Double Takes." *Art in America* (New York), vol. 68, no. 8, Oct., pp. 113-17.

Tatransky, Valentin. "Cindy Sherman." *Arts Magazine* (New York), vol. 54, no. 10, June, p. 77.

1981
Allen Memorial Art Museum, Oberlin College, Ohio. *Young Americans*, Apr. 1-May 3. Catalogue, text by Douglas Crimp, Joanna Frueh, William Olander and Carter Ratcliff.

Cohen, Ronny H. "Love is Blind." *Artforum* (New York), vol. 20, no. 2, Oct., pp. 82-83.

Crimp, Douglas. "The Photographic Activity of Postmodernism." *October* (Cambridge, Massachusetts), no. 15, Winter, pp. 91-101.

Elliott, David. "Photography — Two Artists Views: Splendid Churches and Witty Sexuality." *Chicago Sun-Times* (Chicago), Dec. 13, Show section, p. 14.

Flood, Richard. "Cindy Sherman: Metro Pictures." *Artforum* (New York), vol. 19, no. 7, Mar., p. 80.

Frueh, Joanna. "Young Americans at the Allen Memorial Art Museum." *Art in America* (New York), vol. 69, no. 8, Oct., p. 151.

Grundberg, Andy. "Cindy Sherman: A Playful and Political Post Modernist." *The New York Times* (New York), Nov. 22, section 2, p. 35.

Hayden Gallery, Massachusetts Institute of Technology, Cambridge. *Body Language: Figurative Aspects of Recent Art*, Oct. 2-Dec. 24. Catalogue, text by Roberta Smith. Traveled to The Fort Worth Art Museum, Texas, Sept. 11-Oct. 24, 1982; University of South Florida Art Gallery, Tampa, Nov. 12-Dec. 17, 1982; Contemporary Arts Center, Cincinnati, Ohio, Jan. 13-Feb. 27, 1983.

1981 (continued)

Karmel, Pepe. "Art/Photography." *The Soho Weekly News* (New York), Nov. 24-30, p. 56.

Klein, Michael. "Cindy Sherman." *Arts Magazine* (New York), vol. 55, no. 7, Mar., p. 5.

Lawson, Thomas. "Last Exit: Painting." *Artforum* (New York), vol. 20, no. 2, Oct., pp. 40-47.

Lifson, Ben. "Fashionable Features." *The Village Voice* (New York), Dec. 2, p. 102.

Rheinisches Landesmuseum, Bonn, West Germany. *Lichtbildnisse: The Portrait in Photography*, Mar. 1-June 1. Catalogue, text by Klaus Honnef.

Smith, Roberta. "Art: Spacewalk." *The Village Voice* (New York), Nov. 18, p. 98.

Thomas, Lew and d'Agostino, Peter, ed. *Still Photography: the problematic model.* San Francisco: NFS Press, pp. 18-21.

Zelevansky, Lynn. "Cindy Sherman, Metro Pictures." *Flash Art* (Milan, Italy), no. 102, Mar.-Apr., p. 43.

1982

Contemporary Arts Center, Cincinnati, Ohio. *Face It: 10 Contemporary Artists*, July 8-Aug. 28. Catalogue, texts by William Olander and Joanna Frueh. Organized by the Ohio Foundation on the Arts. Traveled to The Museums at Hartwick College, Oneonta, New York, Sept. 12-Oct. 16; The College of Wooster Art Museum, Ohio, Oct. 24-Nov. 21; Contemporary Art Center at Cleveland, Ohio, Dec. 3-Jan. 3, 1983; Trisolini Gallery, Ohio University, Athens, Jan. 10-Feb. 12, 1983; University of Colorado Art Galleries, Boulder, Mar. 5-Apr. 9, 1983; Freedman Galleries, Albright College, Reading, Pennsylvania, Mar. 17-June 19, 1983; Doane Hall Art Gallery, Allegheny College, Meadville, Pennsylvania, Oct. 20-Nov. 18, 1983; Southern Ohio Museum and Cultural Center, Portsmouth, Dec. 18, 1983-Jan. 28, 1984.

Galerie Déjà Vu, Dijon, France. *Cindy Sherman*, Oct. 25-Nov. 13. Catalogue, statement by and interview with the artist.

Gambrell, Jamey. "Cindy Sherman, Metro Pictures." *Artforum* (New York), vol. 20, no. 6, Feb., pp. 85-86.

Glueck, Grace. "Cindy Sherman." *The New York Times* (New York), Oct. 22, p. C22.

Goldberg, RoseLee. "Post-TV Art." *Portfolio* (New York), vol. 55, no. 4, July-Aug., pp. 76-79.

Grundberg, Andy. "Photography View: Crossovers with the Art World." *The New York Times* (New York), Sept. 12, p. 33.

Howell, John and Rice, Shelley. "Cindy Sherman's Seductive Surfaces." *Alive Magazine* (New York), vol. 1, no. 2, Sept.-Oct., pp. 20-25.

Institute of Contemporary Art, University of Pennsylvania, Philadelphia. *Image Scavengers: Photography*, Dec. 8-Jan. 30, 1983. Catalogue, text by Paula Marincola and Douglas Crimp.

Kassel, West Germany. *Documenta 7.* Catalogue.

Knight, Christopher. "Photographer with an Eye on Herself." *Los Angeles Herald Examiner* (Los Angeles), Oct. 10, p. E5.

Kuspit, Donald. "The Night Mind." *Artforum* (New York), vol. 21, no. 1, Sept., pp. 64-67.

Larson, Kay. "Art." *New York Magazine* (New York), Nov. 8, p. 73.

Linker, Kate. "Melodramatic Tactics." *Artforum* (New York), vol. 21, no. 1, Sept., pp. 30-32.

Milwaukee Art Museum, Wisconsin. *New Figuration in America*, Dec. 3-Jan. 23, 1983. Catalogue, texts by Russell Bowman and Peter Schjeldahl.

Phillips, Donna-Lee. "Recent Color: The Contemporary Concern." *Artweek* (Oakland, California), Sept. 25, pp. 1, 16.

Ratcliff, Carter. "Contemporary American Art." *Flash Art* (Milan, Italy), no. 108, Summer, pp. 32-35.

The Renaissance Society at the University of Chicago, Illinois. *A Fatal Attraction: Art and the Media*, May 2-June 12. Catalogue, text by Thomas Lawson.

Rhodes, Richard. "Cindy Sherman's 'Film Stills'." *Parachute* (Montreal, Quebec, Canada), no. 28, Sept.-Oct.-Nov., pp. 4-7.

Ristorcelli, Jacques and Pouvreau, Paul. "Les Auto-Portraits de Cindy Sherman." *Cahiers du Cinéma* (Paris, France), Feb., pp. 13-14.

Roberts, John. "The Art of Self-Attention." *Artscribe* (London, England), no. 36, Aug., pp. 50-55.

Schjeldahl, Peter. "Curator Cure Thyself." *The Village Voice* (New York), May 18, p. 87.

_____. "Shermanettes." *Art in America* (New York), vol. 70, no. 3, Mar., pp. 110-11.

Stedelijk Museum, Amsterdam, The Netherlands. *Cindy Sherman*, Dec. 24-Jan. 1983. Catalogue, text by Els Barents.

Walker Art Center, Minneapolis, Minnesota. *Eight Artists: The Anxious Edge*, Apr. 25-June 13. Catalogue, text by Lisa Lyons.

Whitney Museum of American Art, Downtown Branch, New York. *Frames of Reference*, May 6 - June 4. Catalogue, text by Nora Halpern.

1983

Art Gallery, Fine Arts Center, State University of New York at Stony Brook. *Cindy Sherman*, Oct. 1-Nov. 2. Catalogue, text by Thom Thompson. Traveled to Center for the Fine Arts, Wesleyan University, Middletown, Connecticut, Nov. 9-Dec. 16.

Ashbery, John. "Biennials Bloom in the Spring." *Newsweek* (New York), Apr. 18, pp. 93-94.

Center Gallery, Bucknell University, Lewisburg, Pennsylvania. *Faces Since the 50's*, Mar. 11-Apr. 17. Catalogue, text by Joseph Jacobs.

Cohen, Ronny. "Star Quality." *Portfolio* (New York), vol. 5, no. 5, Sept.-Oct., pp. 80-87.

Davis, Douglas. "Big Pix." *Newsweek* (New York), May 2, pp. 80-81, 84.

Dimitrijevic, Nena. "Urban Kisses, Institute of Contemporary Arts." *Flash Art* (Milan, Italy), no. 110, Jan., p. 66.

Glueck, Grace. "Artists Who 'Scavenge' from the Media." *The New York Times* (New York), Jan. 9, pp. H29-30.

Goldberg, Vicki. "Portrait of a Photographer as a Young Artist." *The New York Times* (New York), Oct. 23, section 2, p. 29.

Grundberg, Andy. "Photography: Biennial Show." *The New York Times* (New York), Apr. 1, p. C23.

_____. "Post-Modernists in the Mainstream." *The New York Times* (New York), Nov. 20, section C, p. 27.

Hapgood, Susan. "Cindy Sherman, Metro Pictures/New York." *Flash Art* (Milan, Italy), no. 110, Jan., p. 63.

Halley, Peter. "A Note on the 'New Expressionism' Phenomenon." *Arts Magazine* (New York), vol. 57, no. 7, Mar., pp. 88-89.

Hirshhorn Museum and Sculpture Garden, Washington, D.C. *Directions 1983*, Mar. 10-May 15. Catalogue, text by Phyllis D. Rosenzweig.

Karmel, Pepe. "Photography: Looking at the Big Picture." *Art in America* (New York), vol. 71, no. 7, Sept., pp. 35-39.

Larson, Kay. "Beyond Pure Photography." *New York Magazine* (New York), May 2, pp. 73-75.

Levin, Kim. "Double Takes." *The Village Voice* (New York), Apr. 26, p. 91.

Lichtenstein, Therese. "Cindy Sherman." *Arts Magazine* (New York), vol. 57, no. 5, Jan., p. 3.

Linker, Kate. "Cindy Sherman, Metro Pictures." *Artforum* (New York), vol. 21, no. 5, Jan., p. 79.

Marzorati, Gerald. "Imitation of Life." *Art News* (New York), vol. 82, no. 7, Sept., pp. 78-87, cover.

Musée d'Art et d'Industrie de Saint-Etienne, France. *Cindy Sherman*, Mar.-Apr. Catalogue, text by Christian Caujolle.

Nilson, Lisbet. "Making It Neo." *Art News* (New York), vol. 82, no. 7, Sept., pp. 62-70.

_____. "Q & A: Cindy Sherman." *American Photographer* (New York), Sept., pp. 70-77.

Schjeldahl, Peter. "Falling in Style, The New Art and Our Discontents." *Vanity Fair* (New York), vol. 46, no. 1, Mar., pp. 115-17.

Starenko, Michael. "What's an Artist to Do? A Short History of Postmodernism and Photography." *Afterimage* (New York), vol. 10, no. 6, Jan., pp. 4-5.

The St. Louis Art Museum, Missouri. *Cindy Sherman: Unidentified Photographs*, Mar. 1-Apr. 10. Catalogue, text by Jack Cowart.

Whitney Museum of American Art, New York. *1983 Biennial Exhibition*, Mar. 15-May 22. Catalogue.

Zelevansky, Lynn. "Cindy Sherman, Metro Pictures." *Art News* (New York), vol. 82, no. 1, Jan., pp. 146, 148.

1984

Artists Space, New York. *A Decade of New Art*, May 31-June 30. Catalogue, text by Linda L. Cathcart.

Cohn, Michele. "Cindy Sherman, Metro Pictures." *Flash Art* (Milan, Italy), no. 116, Mar., p. 39.

Gambrell, Jamey. "Marginal Acts." *Art in America* (New York), vol. 72, no. 3, Mar., pp. 114-19.

Grundberg, Andy. "The New Modern Reenters the Contemporary Arena." *The New York Times* (New York), May 27, pp. 27, 32.

Handy, Ellen. "Cindy Sherman." *Arts Magazine* (New York), vol. 58, no. 5, Jan., p. 56.

La Jolla Museum of Contemporary Art, California. *American Art Since 1970*, Mar. 10-Apr. 22. Catalogue, text by Richard Marshall. Organized by the Whitney Museum of American Art, New York. Traveled to Museo Tamayo, Mexico City, Mexico, May 17-July 29; North Carolina Museum of Art, Raleigh, Sept. 29-Nov. 25; Sheldon Memorial Art Gallery, University of Nebraska, Lincoln, Jan. 12-Mar. 3, 1985; Center for the Fine Arts, Miami, Florida, Mar. 30-May 26, 1985.

Liebmann, Lisa. "Cindy Sherman, Metro Pictures." *Artforum* (New York), vol. 22, no. 7, Mar., p. 95.

Naef, Weston and Rathbone, Belinda, ed. *The Gallery of World Photography/New Directions*. Tokyo, Japan: Shueisha Publishing Co., Inc., pp. 23, 203.

Ravenal, John B. "Cindy Sherman." *Arts Magazine* (New York), vol. 58, no. 5, Jan., p. 21.

Robotham, Rosemarie. "One-Woman Show: Cindy Sherman Puts Her Best Faces Forward." *Life Magazine* (New York), vol. 7, no. 6, June, pp. 14-15.

Schjeldahl, Peter and Danoff, I. Michael. *Cindy Sherman*. New York: Pantheon Books.

Seibu Gallery of Contemporary Art, Tokyo, Japan. *Cindy Sherman*, Mar.-Apr. Catalogue.

Smith, Roberta. "We Remember MOMA: Temporary Misgivings." *The Village Voice* (New York), May 22, pp. 89, 92.

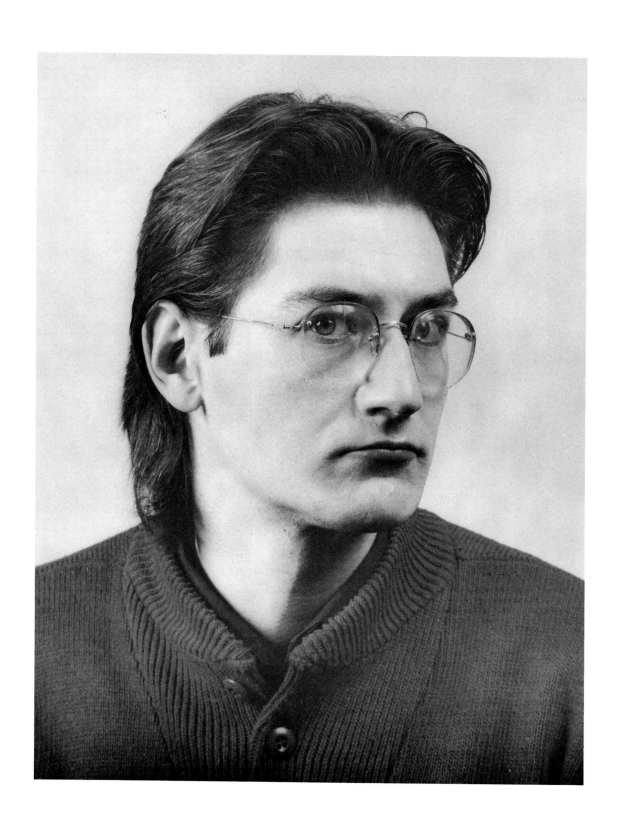

Michael Zwack
photograph by Robert Mapplethorpe, March 1983

Michael Zwack

I am not concerned with mere reportage. These images evoke rather than specify, triggering within the viewer personal memories and associations. This non-specific depiction, combined with a particular style and execution reduces the descriptive quality of the source image (usually a magazine photograph) and forces a personal interpretation.

I begin by projecting the found image and rubbing raw pigment directly into the surface of the paper. After several layers of colors are applied, I wash the painting with oil, creating a veiled image. Incidents surrounding the image are not represented. People are isolated from their stories and presented again in a transitional moment. The image becomes disconnected from a historical time frame. The image must provoke emotion without describing an event.

It is memory and the mind's ability to associate that creates the narrative peculiar to the person standing before the work.

The Last Great Performance 1981
Raw pigment and oil on paper
76 x 71 in. (193.04 x 180.34 cm.)
Collection Dannheisser Foundation

Untitled 1982
Raw pigment and oil on paper
79 x 50 in. (200.66 x 127 cm.)
Courtesy Metro Pictures, New York

Untitled 1982
Raw pigment and oil on paper
57¹/₂ x 87¹/₄ in. (146.05 x 221.62 cm.)
Courtesy Metro Pictures, New York

Michael Zwack

One-Artist Exhibitions
1974
Gallery 219, State University College, Buffalo, New York.

HALLWALLS, Buffalo, New York.

1977
Essex Art Center, Buffalo, New York.

1979
Artists Space, New York.

1980
Studio d'Arte, Cannaviello, Milan, Italy.

1981
Metro Pictures, New York.

1982
Metro Pictures, New York.

1983
Gallery Now, Stockholm, Sweden.

Gallery Christofferson, Norway.

1984
Texas Gallery, Houston.

Selected Readings
1976
Willig, Nancy Tobin. "Buffalo: Typestyles and photographic manipulations." *Art News* (New York), vol. 75, no. 8, Oct., pp. 106-08.

1979
Cathcart, Linda L. "The Western Image in New York: Longo, Sherman, Zwack." *Arts Quarterly* (New Orleans, Louisiana), no. 1, Oct.-Nov.-Dec., pp. 8-9.

Upton Gallery, State University College, Buffalo, New York. *HALLWALLS: 5 Years*, Nov. 5-15. Catalogue, text by Linda L. Cathcart. Organized by The New Museum, New York. Traveled to A Space, Toronto, Ontario, Canada, Feb. 16-Mar. 8, 1980; Parsons School of Art Gallery, New York, June 20-July 18, 1980.

1980
Brooke Alexander Inc., New York. *Illustration & Allegory*, May 13-June 14. Catalogue, text by Carter Ratcliff.

Phillips, Deborah C. "Reviews: Illustration & Allegory." *Arts Magazine* (New York), vol. 55, no. 1, Sept., pp. 25-26.

Rickey, Carrie. "Babes on West Broadway." *The Village Voice* (New York), July 9, p. 62.

Simon, Joan. "Double Takes." *Art in America* (New York), vol. 68, no. 8, Oct., pp. 113-17.

Tatransky, Valentin. "Illustration & Allegory." *Arts Magazine* (New York), vol. 55, no. 1, Sept., p. 4.

1981
Tatransky, Valentin. "Death or Glory." *Cover* (New York), no. 5, Spring-Summer, pp. 42-47.

_____. "Fischl, Lawson, Robinson, and Zwack: they make pictures." *Arts Magazine* (New York), vol. 55, no. 10, June, pp. 147-49.

_____. "Richard Prince/Michael Zwack." *Arts Magazine* (New York), vol. 55, no. 9, May, p. 34.

1982
Contemporary Arts Center, Cincinnati, Ohio. *Face It: 10 Contemporary Artists*, July 8-Aug. 28. Catalogue, texts by William Olander and Joanna Frueh. Organized by the Ohio Foundation on the Arts. Traveled to The Museums at Hartwick College, Oneonta, New York, Sept. 12-Oct. 16; The College of Wooster Art Museum, Ohio, Oct. 24-Nov. 21; Contemporary Art Center of Cleveland, Ohio, Dec. 3-Jan. 3, 1983; Trisolini Gallery, Ohio University, Athens, Jan. 10-Feb. 12, 1983; University of Colorado Art Galleries, Boulder, Mar. 5-Apr. 9, 1983; Freedman Galleries, Albright College, Reading, Pennsylvania, Mar. 17-June 19, 1983; Southern Ohio Museum and Cultural Center, Portsmouth, Dec. 18, 1983-Jan. 28, 1984.

Goldberg, RoseLee. "Post-TV Art." *Portfolio* (New York), vol. 4, no. 4, July-Aug., pp. 76-79.

Greenspan, Stuart. "Galleries: Art on the Edge." *Art & Auction* (New York), July-Aug., p. 30.

Hayden Gallery, Massachusetts Institute of Technology, Cambridge. *Great Big Drawings*, Apr. 3-May 2. Catalogue, text by Katy Kline.

Kuspit, Donald. "Critical Perspectives at P.S. 1." *Artforum* (New York), vol. 20, no. 8, Apr., pp. 81-82.

Tatransky, Valentin. "Michael Zwack." *Arts Magazine* (New York), vol. 57, no. 1, Sept., p. 38.

1983
Armstrong, Richard. "Other Views." *Artforum* (New York), vol. 22, no. 4, Dec., p. 83.

Bannon, Anthony. "Image Scavengers." *The Buffalo News* (Buffalo), July 1, Gusto section, pp. 3, 14.

Kirshner, Judith Russi. "Compassionate Images, N.A.M.E. Gallery." *Artforum* (New York), vol. 21, no. 9, May, pp. 102-03.

1984
Artists Space, New York. *A Decade of New Art*, May 31-June 30. Catalogue, text by Linda L. Cathcart.

Cotter, Holland. "Civilization and the Landscape of Discontent." *Arts Magazine* (New York), vol. 58, no. 10, Summer, p. 40.

Everingham, Carol J. "Critic's Choice: New View of World." *The Houston Post* (Houston), June 15, p. E2.

Indianapolis Museum of Art, Indiana. *Painting and Sculpture Today 1984*, May 1-June 10. Catalogue, text by Helen Ferrulli.

Johnson, Patricia C. "Furniture as art on view, and new artist debuts." *Houston Chronicle* (Houston), June 8, section 5, p. 1.

Larson, Kay. "Fresh Faces for Summer." *New York Magazine* (New York), June 25, pp. 54-55.

The Museum of Modern Art, New York. *An International Survey of Recent Painting and Sculpture*, May 17-Aug. 19. Catalogue.

Russell, John. "Art: Inaugural Show at Museum is Survey of Works from All Over." *The New York Times* (New York), May 18, p. 23.

Staff

Board of Trustees

Photograph Credits
Numerals refer to page numbers

D. James Dee, 62 (lower).
Albert Dundler, 40 (lower).
eeva-inkeri, 55.
Xavier Fourcade, Inc., 38, 39.
Rick Gardner, 46, 47, 52.
Judy Linn, 40 (upper).
© Robert Mapplethorpe, 72, 73, 74, 75, 76, 77.
Pelka/Noble, 44, 45, 67, 121, 122.
Eric Pollitzer, New York, 22, 23, 24.
Steven Sloman Fine Arts Photography, 53, 54.
Ivan Dalla Tana, 25.
Alan Zindman, 102.
Zindman/Fremont, 61, 92, 93, 94, 100, 101.

Design by **Creel Morrell Inc.**; Houston, Texas
1000 copies printed by **Printmasters, Inc.**; Austin, Texas
Typesetting by **Typographic Resources**; Houston, Texas